Just an intentionally blank page, nothing to see here, move along.

~ 1 ~

ISBN 978-1490453040
Library of Congress cataloging in Publication data is on file at the Library of Congress, Washington DC

Yes, another blank page! I can't believe how much I'm spending to print blank pages.

OUR SEMI VIEW

Leslie Adams Rogers

Don't worry; this page has been left blank intentionally.

Something to do with chapters starting on an odd numbered page.

Yup, this page too. You have not missed any words of wisdom.

They are next

Now I Know

Why Truckers Swear,

They Are Driven To It

OUR SEMI VIEW

Once upon a time......well maybe.
It was a dark and stormy night.....at times.
Call me Ishmael.....not a chance.
It was the best of times, it was the worst of times.....true

Oh who am I trying to fool, this is not going to be the next great American novel. It's just my story. My Semi View from a semi-truck. All this started out as blogs to try and keep family and friends up to date on where we were and what we were doing. It was a difficult decision to make, to begin truck driving. But the bill collectors helped convince me it was the right thing to do.

In the end, we accomplished what we set out to do. Get caught up on bills, downsize and getting rid of the house payment. Now it is time for us to quit driving and enjoy our severely missed family and friends.

Before you start reading this, I should warn you about my writing style. It is a little unconventional. I write as if I were sitting across from you telling you the story. As happens often when someone is telling a story, there are times I go on and on. And on. Sometimes I used the blog as a sounding board, a place to vent my frustrations. Sometimes like a Dear Diary. Often as a soap box.

I could not put every blog into this book or every picture. I had to pick and choose which blogs to include here. I tried to choose the ones that everyone liked best. The funny ones, the frustrating ones. Not being there when your kids are going through rough, life changing events, or even the joyful times. A phone call or a text is not the same as a hug and a kiss.

This book was not professionally edited, spell checked or grammar corrected. So I apologize in advance if I missed something that appears so obvious, you are thinking how could I have missed it?

I hope you enjoy my stories as much as I enjoy sharing the experience.

Leslie

Getting Started

Well here I am about to start a new chapter in my life. Chapter 10, truck driver.

Chapter 1: Childhood. Being the oldest of 6, that was a long and interesting chapter.
Chapter 2: Motherhood. Paige is the star character in this chapter of my life.
Chapter 3: Marriage and divorce. A short but necessary chapter.
Chapter 4: New love, new challenges. My husband Will and second daughter Jennifer help write this chapter.
Chapter 5: Ten years later our son Willy rounds out our family.
Chapter 6: Life, love and marriage. Just life as we know it.
Chapter 7: Grown kids. The girls get married
Chapter 8: Grand kids. Kenny, Mariah, Natelie and Lilly. This is the best chapter and I hope it gets so big it needs its own book.
Chapter 9: Gains and losses. Lost my job, but gained a sense of who my friends are and what family really means.
Chapter 10: Truck driving mama-Just making entries into this chapter.

After tearing my rotator cuff, I had to find a new job. I got my school bus driving endorsement. There is a lot to driving a bunch of kids around. Because I get lost so easy, I would go to the bus barn the day before and get my route and drive it in my car making notes; The 3rd driveway is really the 4th set of mail boxes. There is no street sign for D Street; it is not after E street. Stop at big Cotton Wood tree. It didn't bother me the yelling and screaming. Coming from a big family immunized me from hearing those noises.

On one of my first trips I learned we are supposed to make sure that all kindergarteners are picked up by an adult. But in my defense, I didn't know who was in kindergarten and who is in first grade. After letting several kids off, I close the doors and get ready to pull away. One little girl comes up to me and says "Matthew is not supposed to get off here" Who's Matthew? So in a split second I have to decide do I just ignore her, after all she's just a kid. Leave Matthew to nature, survival of the fittest. Or leave a bus load of kids to chase this Matthew down the street. I look at the back of the bus and pick out the class clown, one of the older kids, and tell him to come up here. I said you're in charge, make sure everyone stays seated. Why did I pick the joker? Because everyone already pays attention to him and he would be thrilled to be recognized and put in a position of authority. I turn the bus off, grab the keys, step one foot off the bus, and in my loudest mom voice yell "MATTHEW!" He stops, looks back at me and I crook my finger for him to come back. The universal mom signal that every kid understands. I asked him if this is his stop. He shook his head no. I asked then why did you get off? He just shrugged his shoulders and got back on the bus.

But that was not even the biggest problem. I hated having to drive for 5 minutes, look for an address. I just always felt lost. I was only working as a substitute driver, which gave me about 3 hours a week. This didn't pay any bills.

So it seemed to Will and I (mostly Will) the next logical step would be for me to get my CDL class A license and we could become team drivers. Our plan was to work for the company Will was already driving for. After I went to school and got my license his employer told him they couldn't get around the insurance requirement of 2 years' experience. They hoped that Will's 25 years' experience would sway the insurance company. They did not sway or even bend. Bummer. The next company I went to I didn't pass the backing test. Bummer. So now we are heading off to another trucking company. Will is already there and I am about to start. I've been trying to figure out what to bring. 8 pants, 14 shirts, 14 under pants, shoes, socks, towels, bathroom gear, oh my gosh that is a whole bag by itself. The powders, soap deodorant, make up hair stuff, curling iron, hair blower, etc.

Food. I have to think carefully about this part. My IBS won't let me eat just anything, especially since the bathroom is more than 10 feet away. So let's see, crackers, rice, ok food is taken care of.

Music. Even though we have Sirius radio in the truck I'd better take along my favorites, Jimmy Buffett, John Butler Trio, Maria Muldaur, Warren Zevon, Bonnie Rait, and The Uppity Blues Woman.
Other Entertainment: I'll have to look through my book case to see what books I can read again. Pillars of the Earth, World without End,

The Shack, I cry every time I read that one. Or maybe one I haven't read yet. I have to remember to grab a couple of movies. Will already has his favorites but I don't need to list those titles, I'm sure you can guess.

I don't think I can bring my belly dance instructor. But I should grab a cd so I can listen to the music and visualize my moves. I will tell you, for most of our time together, whenever I would come home and say to Will, 'Honey I'm going to take water aerobics', 'I'm going to take yoga', 'I'm going to sell Tupperware', Will would say, OK if that's what makes you happy, (happy wife, happy life). But the day I came home and said 'Honey, I want to take up Belly Dancing', he became a lot more involved with my activities. How much do you need? Where can you get the outfits? You know very Supportive.

What if I get tired of reading? Maybe I should bring a craft project. What about a crochet or knitting. I'll have to see what I have that I haven't finished. I guess I should wrap this up. I have a lot to do before I hit the road. Mostly, slimming down my list of things to take. I can't really take all that stuff. I need to Shampoo the carpets, knock down the spider webs, pull weeds, wash windows, and show someone how to work the vacuum, dish washer and clothes washer. Make the broom and mop a little more visible.

Our son is a senior in High School this year. He will be living the dream, home alone while mom and dad travel the country side. He has to take care of the dog. Sergeant Schultz ruptured his Achilles tendon, behind his hock on his rear right foot. That's not what it is called on a dog, but that's what it is equal to for us. He can't bear weight on it. So he has been tri-poding around here for quite a while. He's getting weekly shots for inflammation and daily pills for pain. The vet said the only way to fix it and bring back the integrity of the tendon is to go to an orthopedic surgeon. He will have to live with his brace.

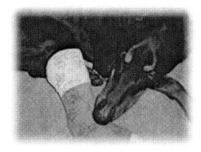

Well I hope this blog works out. I'll see how often I get around to posting. Hope it's a good way to let you all know where we are and what we're doing. I hope it helps to easy my family's mind over my lack of directional skills. I also have dyslexia. And not the, Oh that's cute she made her E look like a 3, dyslexia. The teacher sends a note home saying I think we have a problem. I have to put Leslie's work up to a mirror to correct it. I went to a special school and they retrained my brain. Will and I talked a lot before taking this leap of faith. He has adamantly assured me that I don't need to know where I'm going, I need to know how to follow directions. Which he seems to think I can do.

Buckle up; it's going to be a bumpy ride.

Love and miss you all.

First Rule

Will stopped at a rest area for a bathroom break. After Will went in I decided I would go in too. I hate to pass up a bathroom. When I came out of the bathroom I see Will getting in the truck and he starts it and then starts to write in his log book. I opened the door and climbed in. Will looked startled. He said he didn't know I was gone. He thought I was still in the sleeper.

So, new rule. When you go back to the sleeper leave your shoes up front. If your shoes are here, you are here.

Love and miss you all

Omak Suicide Race

After a very windy night in Kennewick Washington, we are off to make our Home Depot deliveries. Kennewick, Richland, Moses Lake and Omak. Along the way we are hoping to find a Wal-Mart so we can pick up a few supplies. Number one on the list Diet Pepsi Vanilla. The last Wal-Mart did not have any so I had to settle for Diet Dr. Pepper. And we need more bottled water too.

So far everyone has been nice, no big problems. One nice man even offered me a cookie, after he gave me crap while I was backing up and parking. After I did it right he came back on the CB and said "Well, well give the little lady a cookie". It makes Will more nervous when I park than it makes me. I know I'm learning, but Will doesn't want me putting up with all the negative comments, he usually turns the CB off when I start to park, but he forgot that time. We are in Omak Washington; we probably won't get a reload out of here, so looks like we are here for 34 hours. We did get to a Wal-Mart and yes they did have Diet Vanilla Pepsi.

Omak is famous ~if that's what you want to call it~ for the Omak Suicide Race. It's going on this weekend. It involves horses and riders. They start with a 120 foot, full gallop, the horses and riders continue down a 210 foot downhill at a 62 degree angle. After a panicked swim of more than 100 yards the horses face the final grueling uphill sprint. Over the past 25 years 20 horses have died. For the life of me I don't know why any town would want this as their claim to fame. Needless to say we won't be enjoying any local events on these 34 hours off. We'll just hang out at the truck stop. Hope everyone is doing well.

Love and miss you all,

Get out of Denver Baby, Go-Go

While driving to New Mexico we passed a lot of sights in Arizona. We passed the exit for Sedona AZ, the spiritual and metaphysical mecca for hippies and gypsies. We passed the exit for meteor crater, the best preserved meteorite crater on earth.

We passed the Petrified Forest National Park, the world's largest and most colorful concentration of petrified wood. We also passed both the Grand Canyon and Walnut Canyon; (probably grand in its own right) I40 would be a great route for a vacation.

Albuquerque New Mexico is one of the nicest big cities I've been to. The folks are very friendly, polite and helpful. The roads are neat and clean and the town smells so good. The freeway and over passes were framed with coral/terracotta colored cement. It was a lot easier on the eye than staring at white cement full of graffiti.

After we picked up our load we are headed to Denver. It's only 400 miles, not a good pay day, but it is what it is. I hope to get back home soon. I miss everyone. Since I'm driving to Denver I hope I'm better at down shifting going up hills, than I was driving here. I kept missing gears. I ended up stopping on a 7% grade and starting in 1st. A big NO~NO, very dangerous. Will was yelling at me, the drivers behind me were swearing on the CB. The construction workers on the freeway were looking and shaking their heads. Even they know I'm not supposed to be stopping on a hill.

We arrived at our drop off location. Will ended up driving around Aurora, We had a 4:30am appointment, but the guy with the bolt cutters doesn't come on until 6 so they can't cut off the seal until then. Are you kidding me!! So we wait. If it isn't one thing it's another. I asked Will why we don't have bolt cutters. He said he has just never carried them. That way if the trailer is broken into he can say it wasn't him because he doesn't carry bolt cutters. I said if we were going to steal our own load don't you think we would be smart enough to throw the bold cutters away. He didn't answer me

I think Bob Seger was wrong when he sang 'Get out of Denver'. We can't get a load out. The drivers lounge is full. So while we wait we will take advantage of the laundry and showers. Just a little side note, the Denver police force is well funded. There are cops all over the freeway pulling cars over.

We walked to Wal-Mart, just down the street a few blocks, (then through a field and over 2 sets of rail road tracks and across a 4 lane road.)Through the field there were Prairie Dogs and as the path led us close to a mound we  could hear the prairie dog bark ~more like a squeak~ to warn the others about us.
And just as we got close he would duck back in his hole and the next guard would send out his

alert. It took about 5 Prairie dog alerts to cross the field. That was fun to watch, almost as much as Meerkat Manor.

Finally got a load, we are off to Shreveport Louisiana. I'll have to call Sally and Doug for tips on speaking and understanding Cajun.

Oh my gosh, it is hot and humid. The truck stop was full when we got here, about 10pm and we had just decided to park on a side street, when we saw someone leave and we suddenly became parking lot stalkers. But we got the spot. We have not turned the truck off and we are here until Monday. The 1 load of laundry isn't going to get done today. Although there are 4 washers only one is working. And with the humidity it would take 5 times through the dryer I'm sure. But I'm also sure after we deliver in the morning we won't get a load out right away, so I'm hoping there is a regular laundromat down town.

A lot of trucks are hooked up to idle-air. It's a system that gives your truck heat or ac, internet and satellite T.V., without idling, without using your fuel, for a price, of course. It cost between $1.50 and $2.15 an hour depends on where you're at. So spending 34 hours off and hooked up to Idle Air is expensive. Since every state as some law against idling it's kind of a must have business. I don't know why our truck is certified a clean idle vehicle, yet we can't idle. Our semi puts out fewer emissions than your car.

UGH! I can't believe how hot and humid it is here and I can't believe I am the only ones complaining about it.

There is so much going on at home. I wish I could be there. It's very hard to know one of your kids' needs you and all you can say is I'm just a phone call away. But don't call while I'm driving I can't talk. I don't like driving. I wish I could get another job and be there for my kids like a mother should be.

   Hope to get home soon

Love and miss you all

Good Backing Job, Almost

That was quite a thunder storm in Kansas as we were leaving, lots of lightening out this way.

I was trying to back into a spot I picked out. It took me 3-4 pull ups then I thought I was done and somewhat proud of my effort when a guy came on the CB and said "Darlin' all your hard work was for nothing, you're in a hazard material only spot".

I had to move. I found a spot I could just pull thru. (I know that's cheating)

Love and miss you all

Salt Lake City

Leaving Phoenix, finally! The temperature is just unreal, 103. We are picking up empty 2 liter bottles destined for Salt Lake City, Utah. In case anyone was wondering, a truck load of 2 liter bottles is 28,224 bottles. They are going to Coca-Cola. I wish it was going to Pepsi. I want to speak to someone about the availability of Diet Pepsi Vanilla~~rather the lack of availability.

 We see lots of Saguaro Cactus. Did you know they mainly grow in the deserts of Arizona? They are also found in the deserts of Southern California, and the state of Sonora Mexico. The arms begin to grow after the cactus reaches a height of 15 feet, and at least 75 years old. They live to be around 200 years old, can have up to 50 arms and reach a height of 50 feet. The holes are made by the Gila woodpecker

bird, looking for insects and water. They can hold up to a ton of water. Sometimes they get so big and weigh so much that they need help remaining upright.

I also got some top secret pictures of inside the Coca-Cola plant. Very hush-hush, don't tell anyone. One way Coke is trying to sabotage Pepsi, is by stealing their pallets. It's hard to read but among all the pallets marked property of coca cola enterprise Denver, or property of 7 up Reno, there was one pallet that was marked property of Pepsi-Co. (probably should have cases of Diet Pepsi Vanilla)

Love and miss you all

The Legend of the Bear Whisperer is Born

After dropping off FedEx in Seattle, They did not issue us a load right away. When we got our pre-plan it was for Phoenix and they wanted us to drop the trailer in Fresno so we could do FedEx. Because the preplan was sent with a late pick up time we would not be able to do FedEx on Thursday and we would have to sit down in Fresno until Fridays FedEx. We told our driver manager that we cannot afford to sit there. We need to take this load to Phoenix, 1400 miles. Reluctantly she agreed, we were getting shorted miles, and we could take this load to Phoenix.

Everybody knows about my navigational skills, or lack thereof. They are legendary. My inability to find west when looking directly into the setting sun is not just here-say. But when White Trucking sent us directions to Phoenix from Seattle, I had to question them. I thought we should go south on I5 and at some point, maybe around LA or San Diego, turn left towards Phoenix. White Trucking sent us east, then a little west, then east again, then south and finally ending up in Phoenix. Well I'm sure that was there plan anyway.

We went through Washington, Oregon, Idaho, Nevada, and Arizona. I5 seemed much easier, and as it turns out would have been about 188 miles shorter; and by the way, directions should be written; turn at the exit with the watch for deer sign, not the one with buck shot, the sign with the red reflector on the deer's nose, or take the exit immediately after the weight station.

Sadly our son inherited my DCD. Directional Comprehension Disorder is what we call it. It is not yet recognized as a medical disorder, probably because nobody can find the clinic doing the studies. He received a Tom-Tom for Christmas and F.Y.I., a GPS does not qualify as a tax deductible medical expense. Not yet anyway.

We leave Laughlin, NV, headed towards Phoenix. No problem. I'm on 93 south, turn on to 40 east, then onto 93 south again.

I'm driving...and driving...and driving...and yes still driving. When I start to wonder why there is snow again on the roadside, didn't I leave that behind in Idaho? Oh well I don't see my turn.
Driving...driving...driving... Oh look, Little America Truck Stop I remember that place, that's where I got the matching cowgirls outfits for our granddaughters.(cute as heck by the way) so this must be the right direction.

Driving...driving...

Yep, there's the sign for Winslow I remember complaining to Will I wanted to go and stand on  a corner in Winslow Arizona
Driving...driving. Hey it's getting dark, Will said we'd be there by 6 or 7 and I still have lots of turns on my list. Now that I think about it I haven't seen any signs telling the distance to Phoenix for a long, long time.

CRAP! Now I have to wake him up. There's nothing like poking the bear in the middle of hibernation. I wish I had a ten foot pole, but there isn't that much room between us anyway.

Will says where are you?

I don't know, I'm still looking for my turn to Phoenix

Well you're wrong

But I saw Little America and we were there once before.

Yea when we delivered in Flagstaff!!

Winslow, I remember that, remember?

YES on our way to Flagstaff from Los Angles!

**some words were omitted due to inappropriate language **

Turns out Flagstaff is nowhere near Phoenix

I tried to turn around; trying not to make direct eye contact or any sarcastic remarks, history tells me that only irritates the bear. But as it was inevitable my turn around skills were not up to par, so the bear took over. I tried to get out of ear shot, so I didn't have to listen to his growling.

We made our delivery on time, early since it wasn't due for another 32 hours. Guess what? Our reload is the same, Mor Furniture store, Phoenix to Seattle. Yes, it is the reverse route. Pray for me. *note to family, look for my body off route.

I would like to report I did not make any directional mistakes. Thank you for your applause.

Today he was joking about it. Wondering how I could have missed the turn, why it took me so long to figure it out, etc. He said he doesn't know how I find my way from breakfast to dinner every day.

The moral of my story is no matter how much a bear growls if you give him a little honey, he sweetens right up.
Since I'm able to tell the story is proof of my abilities to calm the savage beast.

And the Legend of the Bear Whisperer is born

Love and miss you all.

Truck Stop Humor

I think my shifting is getting better; at least Will is yelling and throwing his hat less. This is probably our fourth trip from L.A to Seattle and I'm feeling more comfortable down shifting when going uphill. I've figured out 20 to 30 thousand pounds is what I like. But boy oh boy, above that 43 -45 thousand pounds, like paper rolls from the mill, I hate shifting with that weight.

Today we changed drivers at the truck stop in Aurora, near Salem. As we got closer to the truck stop a sweet voice came on the CB asking...in her sweetest southern drawl...if anybody was going to Los Angeles. She's been trying to catch a ride all day, and as is my nature, while driving around looking for a place to park, I started sarcastically answering her in my best southern drawl.

Honey, you've been trying all day to get a ride to LA, what is wrong with this world when a working girl can't get a ride. Well bless you're working little heart. Oops I guess it's not your heart that does all the work. Honey, you are just so sweet you're giving me a tooth ache. Tell me sugar, where you're from do they pronounce it skank or whore or are you just a run of the mill lizard.

 Well, you get the idea. Then towards the end of my rant I was saying. Give me a break, that lot lizard needs to get a real job and stop stealing money from the hard working men around here. Her accent is as phony as mine. It's obvious no real man wants her or she wouldn't be pimpin' herself on the CB. What level of hell did Dante put whores on?

I figured all this was in the privacy of our truck. You know, for mine and Will's enjoyment only. But I didn't notice that Will had reached over and was holding down the mic on the CB. So everyone at the truck stop heard me.

The CB traffic was dead silent for at least 1 minute. Then one guy came on and said, "So you think there's going to be any action around here tonight?" Then everybody put they're 2cents in. 'Can't wait to see those two get together'. 'My money's on the driver not the lizard'. 'Get that lizard out of here', Where is that driver, now that's a real woman and she needs a real man, babe you just come on over I'm in the 3rd row, black KW'. 'I'd pay for both of them, together'

Since there are not a lot of women drivers it's hard to remain anonymous on the CB. Needless to say, I didn't go in and use their bathroom. Down the road we went. I guess that will cost me karma points. Will thought it was the funniest thing ever.

It's nice to know that after 27 years Will is finally learning to appreciate my Adams Family since of humor.

Love and miss you all

Never a Dull Moment in Garland Texas

We had our time off in Garland Texas; we were really tired and didn't want to drive to our regular hotel chain, so we stayed at a local dive. This place had nothing. The bed sucked, no in room coffee pot, no swimming pool, noisy customers, no phone book, not even a Gideon's Bible. All we had was a Waffle House, a Mexican Taqueria, a liquor store and a dentist. Will has had a bad tooth for a couple of months. So I dragged him into the dentist and they got him right in. It was just $99. They ground down past the crack and then built it back up. Will said they can do it so cheap because they don't use any novocain. Meanwhile back at the hotel, the guest next door was outside yelling at some guy down the parking lot (we are on the second floor). Then he took off in his Monte Carlo yelling, "Well that's public property not private, honey." Whatever that means. Maybe we should move the bed out of drive by shooting range?

Will decided to walk down to the liquor store. He comes back and tells me this story. First there is no hard liquor sold in Garland, beer and wine only. Then while he was checking out a guy comes in with a hoody on, and hood is up over his head. One guy is dressed just the same standing just outside the door. The guy picks up a candy bar and walks around the store. Will said the clerk, a petite, little Indian gal, looked around nervously. She was putting his stuff in the bag slowly. Will said he was getting very nervous too. And he was taking his time putting his change away, making small talk, hoping the guy would just leave. Then, walking quickly, from out of the back room, came a short, old man. He reaches under the counter and pulls out a hand gun. He lays it on the counter, keeping his hand on the gun and says in a deep voice, "Boy, you need to remove that hood. Now!" Both guys left. Will said what a relief.

He said at first he was a little concerned when the owner brought out a gun. A little? I would have pee'd my pants. After all that it was dinner time. Our room did not have a phone book so I walked down to the office and asked if they had one. She asked why? I said because I want to look for a place to eat dinner. She said there are flyers on the table. Ok, we looked at them and there was no Mexican food places that

~ 32 ~

delivered. Can you believe it, a town in Texas without a Mexican restaurant? So I went back to the desk and told her they didn't have what we were looking for, can we look at the phone book and could she call us a taxi to take us to a restaurant. She said they don't have a phone book someone stole it, and there is no taxi. If we didn't want something from the flyers we could walk to the Taqueria across the street. The menu was written in Spanish but we could still recognize a couple of items. Tacos, beans and rice to go please. We got back to the hotel to eat and the serving size was so small. The flavor was great, but as it was getting dark, and we didn't want to walk across the street for more, we just ordered pizza.

The next morning at 9:30am, we are getting ready to leave and the maid knocks she asks if we need towels or if we are checking out. We told her we are checking out. Then the phone rings, it's the front desk asking if we are checking out or staying another night we told her we are on the way down. When we get the receipt we see that check out time is noon. We had a good 2 more hours. What is the hurry kicking us out.

And to top off a perfect 34 hours off, the batteries on the truck were dead. We contacted White Trucking, they were useless. On hold so long I hung up. I got on line and looked for someone to come give us a jump start. I called 3 different places and none of them would come jump start a semi. We should not have mentioned it was a semi. Will was getting so mad, and yelling "It's just 12 volts. If you can jump start a car, you can jump start a semi!" I finale got a local guy to come out. He says its $95. Ok whatever, just hurry before this fine establishment charges us another day for sitting in the parking lot. He shows up in his personal pickup truck and hooks up the cables and we wait. We tell him the trouble we had getting someone to come out. He said his brother didn't want him to come because there is a lot of work at the shop for him to do and jump start's don't pay that much. Really $95 sounds like a lot to me. He said he used to be a truck driver and knows how hard it is. No kidding.

Love and miss you all

Happy New Year

This New Year has me reflecting on some of the events from the past year.

I am always thankful for family and friends. Without them none of this would be possible. On second thought not sure if I should thank them or blame them. They take care of things at home so we can be away working. They keep me up to date on all the happenings. They give me more moral and spiritual support than I ever imagined I would need. I am truly blessed. I just need to remind myself of that fact more often.

Since I started truck driving I have a new list of things I am thankful for. Small knitting projects, cross stitch, good books, Tetris on my phone, Colgate wisp mini disposable tooth brushes, the increasingly rare Vanilla Diet

Pepsi, I take this for granted in Oregon. A hot shower that last longer than 3 minutes, hand sanitizer, honey crisp apples, peanut butter & Ritz crackers, single serving size jello & fruit, slow cooker liners, a good map program, someone that can drive at night and back up.
 Love and miss you all,

Getting Paid to Haul an Empty Trailer

Will has been driving a truck for 27 plus years. In that time he has seen trucking company's do very odd things. He has hauled 6 mattresses' from Reno to Portland. He has hauled frozen peas in a non-refer truck. He has hauled 2 John Deer Gators across the state. But this one takes the cake. We arrived at Sea-Tac FedEx for our load going to Oakland. We talked to the dock manager and he told us where to wait. It was getting close to our 4 pm pickup time when he came over to us and said there was no freight to put in the trailer. We asked him if freight was late or something. He said no, in fact there are 2 trailers scheduled to go to Oakland. So we called our dispatch, asked what to do. Hey told us to run the load. Take the empty trailer from Seattle to Oakland. Even the gate guards were shaking their heads when we left. The guards joked that they would have to seal the load, don't want any of this good Seattle air escaping before it gets to Oakland.
 So now Will says he has seen everything.

We showed up at FedEx Oakland Airport and everyone there was confused about why we were trying to deliver an empty trailer. The first guard said we were at the wrong gate because we had an empty trailer. We back up and went to the next gate. And that guard kept telling me where to leave the empty trailer. We told him we need to treat this delivery as if it were loaded. Who signs the loaded trailer delivery sheets?

"Empty trailers go over there."
Nobody wanted to sign for the delivery of an empty trailer. Good grief, Can't say that I blame them about being confused.
Anyway, that's done. Now we are sitting here at the Brooks Ranch Restaurant in Fresno.
Mondays is soup and salad bar day at Brooks Ranch. Navy bean and Minestrone. Umm good.

Love and miss you all,

Edwardsville, Kansas

Thought I should let you all know that thanks to karma, Saint Christopher, daily prayers to my patron saint, Saint Anne and 2 GPS; I am happy to report I have not got lost in a while. Thank you, thank you. Please your standing ovation is too much.

After we deliver the load in Kansas City we need to take some time off, because Will hurt his back. When we dropped the trailer at the White Trucking yard I told the lady at the window I needed to take Will to an urgent care, which one is closest?

"UM, I don't know, can't he just wait and see his doctor in the morning?"

UM we don't live here, that's why I asked.

"OH, well the phone book is over there, I don't know where one is".

I said, Oh you don't live here?

"Yes I live here I just never get sick."
Well honey, I've never been to the Oregon State Mental Hospital, but I can tell you where it is.

Any way we find the address, and take off. Getting Will in and out of the semi was fun. He couldn't lift his legs very high so getting in was harder that getting out. It was easier for him to step down, than up. The ER doctor asked

when it hurts, when it feels ok. Will said it hurts when he stands or sits. They said ok sit here.

They gave Will a shot of flexeril (what a baby) and said if he had any more troubles to go to the urgent care. Then they gave me directions to a Walgreen's and a couple of hotels. The hotels were all full, some big Lance Armstrong Live Strong event. We had to make do in the parking lot for one night. They next day people were checking out so we were able to check in.

Monday (3 days later) rolls around and Will isn't any better, if we are going to stay any

longer we need to move to a cheaper hotel. So
we pack up and leave for the Comfort Inn. After
2 more days Will still isn't any better. I ask the
desk clerk if there is an urgent care nearby and
she said yes, just about 4 blocks. I started to call
for a taxi but Will thought it would hurt more
trying to get in and out of a low car. So I drive
the semi to this little urgent care, of course the
parking lot is not set up for semi parking. Even
bobtailing (no trailer) it's still a big truck. But I
manage to crowd my way into a couple of spots.
I help Will out of the truck. We slowly shuffle
across the parking lot, wait in line just to hear,

"This is not an urgent care until 5pm.
Right now it is a doctor's office, do you have an
appointment?"

Are you kidding me, the sign out front
says urgent care.

"Yes ma'am, but not until 5pm".

It doesn't say that on the sign

"No ma'am it's on the door".

Well, I'm sorry, we don't have an
appointment because we don't live here, can
you fit him in?

"Yes ma'am, after 5. There is a 24hr
urgent care about 25 miles away in Shawnee".

Reverse the whole show, shuffle back to
the truck, steady Will as he climbs into the truck
and off we go. As if it were possible, parking is
worse in Shawnee. I trimmed 3 trees in the
parking lot. No charge, you're welcome. I get
there and it is the size of a double wide trailer.
Only 6 parking spots and no off street parking
allowed. I hate this job!!

We get in and after filling out the paper
work she looks it over and says, "We don't do x-

rays here, we send you down the street and they are read in less than 6 hours. Then you would come back for further exam and to discuss treatment plan and ..." Never mind, all that wore Will out we're going back to the hotel.

Two days later I convinced him we should just go back to the first ER. We did and they took x-rays and gave him some pain meds. More flexeril and steroids this time. Within 24 hours he was able to hobble around the hotel room with crutches. I think it's the steroids that are making the difference. Friday I went down to the front desk to pay for Friday, Saturday and Sunday and she tells me they are booked for the weekend. WTH. This trip just keeps getting better. She got us a room at another Comfort Inn a couple of towns over. Load 'em up and move 'em out.

On the bright side, I am able to get a lot of knitting done. I'm trying to finish a sweater for mom.

A couple of more days and Will is feeling well enough to sit up right. So he stops taking the pain pills and the flexeril. We let dispatch know he is good enough to go. And besides we are broke, but they need to give us a solo load because I'll be driving

and Will is going to be sleeping. He needs to go cold turkey from the pain pills and flexeril in the sleeper.

When it was all said and done, we spent 10 days, 3 hotels, 1 urgent care, and 1 doctor's office disguised as an urgent care, 2 ER visits, in and around Edwardsville Kansas.

Love and miss you all.

Wrong Way Driver

We are off to Pennsylvania, to pick up a Proctor and Gamble load and take it to Utah. This trip from the beginning was difficult. The address where we picked up was on State Route 6. Rand McNally GPS, Copilot, Map Quest and PC Milner for trucks could not find it. Finally after process of elimination, looking on line for the location of a P&G in the town of Tunkhannock PA, I got the real address. The name of the roadway we want is "The Grand Army of the Republic Highway. The directions should have said US Route 6, not State Route 6. I was looking for the address on PA Route 6, big difference.

The next fun part was finding where we were going. We were supposed to drop off in Bear River City Utah. No luck. But not as difficult to figure out. The internet quickly gave us the correct address. The town is really called Tremonton Utah. What a mess. What is the Problem? You'd think a company whose entire business is based on arriving at the right address at the right time would have this all worked out. My turn to drive, so far so good. The air conditioner keeps going in and out. It works well at night. But not so good in Arizona or New Mexico. Hope Will can fix that SOON. The CB was pretty quiet, then all of a sudden seemed like 20 drivers wanted to talk at the same time. They were all yelling but they were cutting each other off so I couldn't hear what they were saying. I almost turned it off; I thought it was just another truck driver testosterone contest. But before I reached the volume control, one driver got through loud and clear.

" WEST BOUND, BREAK CHECK! BREAK CHECK! YOU HAVE A FOUR WHEELER EAST BOUND IN THE HAMMER LANE....WEST BOUND YOU HAVE A EAST BOND FOUR WHEELER. GET IN NUMBER ONE LANE, GET IN NUMBER ONE LANE"

.

So that's what we did, every truck, what a sight, seeing a line of semi's swerve the same direction at the same time. And sure enough here comes a red car with an old man in west bound fast lane, going east. All the four-wheelers, (the cars) stopped when all the trucks around them began to slow and change lanes. Then the CB was busy for a little while. Everyone had to tell a story. "..That's the second wrong way four wheeler in three days" "He came right past me on the off ramp headed for the freeway, one time in Rhode Island I saw a semi headed wrong way,..."

Glad I had the CB on that time. Most of the time the other drivers are talking ok, getting info on where the next truck stop is, can I get from there to here. Asking if the next weight station is open, getting a police car report. Sometimes they tell jokes, not nice ones, so that's when I turn it off. I don't do a lot of talking on the CB just listening. Sometimes they yell at a driver who they think is driving the way wrong. Sometimes they want to talk to me, and I'll talk, but they can be rude or cat calling so I turn it off. But glad I didn't turn in off this time.

The rest of my shift was thankfully uneventful. While Will was driving in Nebraska it was so windy and raining so hard. The road was hot from the sun all day, and with the rain hitting it, it was a really strange site, not fog, but steam on the road, and a lot of it. Then all the cars shot over to under a bridge and stopped. Will thought since they all did the same thing maybe on the local radio station they issued a tornado warning. Will listened to the CB and didn't hear anything about it, so just another strange thing in Nebraska.

We delivered in Utah, no problem. Now we pick up a load of freeze dried food and take it to a Cabela's outdoor store in West Virginia.

Love and miss you all

Thank You Mr. C.O.O

UGH! A while ago White Trucking stacked us with 3 loads. Of course the first 2 sucked but they got us to the good load. We were bobtailing and looking for an empty trailer. First we were to pick up an empty trailer at the Houston Rail Yard and take it to the Bay Town Wal-Mart. The rail yard said they only allowed one driver in at a time, so they wanted Will to wait at the gate. He's in the sleeper, tired from being up all night waiting for a load. Legally if he leaves the sleeper he has to log it. But he usually doesn't. Then he has to split the sleeper time and depending on how long it takes me, he may not have had the right amount of time off to start driving again when we need to switch drivers. I contacted our DM and ask her what to do before I wake Will up. She says just forget drive the 27 miles to Bay Town and get our load from Wal-Mart going to Jenks Oklahoma. When I got to Baytown, Wal-Mart would not let me in without a trailer. I called to tell our DM and she said, what a mess just bobtail to Jenks (510 miles) and get our load to Newark. I agreed, what a mess, but said nothing that happens in Texas surprises me.

When we got our settlement check and those miles from Houston to Baytown to Jenks we not listed. Our DM said Lancaster Terminal (Texas) listed them as unauthorized miles. She said she would look into it. Not authorized! I did every dispatch they sent me. I didn't decide to waste a whole day sightseeing around Texas and Oklahoma. Eventually, (about 2 months), I sent a letter to everyone I could find an email address for. Our terminal manager, the Lancaster manager, the regional manager, and the COO. He got back to me the very next day, both by email and phone call, and said he would look into it. At first I thought he was just trying to appease a disgruntled driver. But next week those 500 miles were on our settlement check. I don't know why the big boss has to get involved before someone does the right thing. Maybe I should keep him on speed dial.

Love and miss you all

When is South not South

I start driving in Hooker Oklahoma. I don't even want to know how they got their name. I'm driving just fine, following directions. I got into Kansas and so far so good except the air conditioner didn't work. Will said it freezes up, that makes no sense to me, then why does it blow warm air. It happens every once in a while so we bought a fan that plugs into the cigarette lighter. I had to find a rest room; I needed to grab the fan and Will's wallet for the upcoming tolls. I get on the toll road from 50 East, my directions say to take 35 South. Will must have heard me say have a nice day to the toll booth lady and he yells from the sleeper:
WHY ARE YOU A TOLL ROAD.
Because that's what it says.
YOU SHOULD BE ON I 35.

~ 44 ~

I am and it's a toll.

HOW DID YOU GET HERE?

From 50 east.

WELL THAT'S NOT RIGHT, SOUTH FROM KANSAS IS OKLAHOMA. THAT'S GOING THE WRONG WAY, WHATS YOUR MILEAGE COUNTER SAY.

(Our GPS counts down the miles to our destination) I told him it's going down.

WELL THAT'S WRONG, WHAT DID YOU DO, WHERES YOUR INSTRUCTIONS, YOUR GOING TO HAVE TO TURN AROUND BEFORE YOU #@%$ EVERYTHING.

I'm following directions!!!

WELL IT'S WRONG

I said, "Listen Will don't start yelling at me for followng your directions. You write them down not me. You yell and scream and swear when I make a mistake, I sure as hell am not going put up with it this time. You are the one that made a mistake not me". He looks at the map, at the directions from White Trucking, then on the lap top, and finally he said White Trucking screwed up. He sent them a message saying the direction should read 35 North. He never said sorry for getting mad at me. I didn't feel like mentioning, he re wrote them for me. I HATE THIS JOB!!

We did avoid a big back up before St Louis. The scoop from the CB said it involved a U-Haul van, a pickup truck and a horse trailer. They had to close the freeway for life flight. The accident was on west bound side, but they had to close east bound too. No sign of anything when we drove by. Glad we missed that one. We've seen quite a few accidents. Mostly just fender benders spin outs from rain or snow. A semi tip over taking a corner to fast or having to stop short and the car behind the truck is so close it hits the truck. Drafting does not work people. When we deliver this tomorrow, we will need to take our 34 hours off. I'll only have about 5 hours left to work and that really doesn't get us anywhere. I hate to lose a good Sunday traveling day; we might be able to get out of New Jersey.

We did end up staying overnight in New Jersey. We ordered Chinese for lunch then for dinner pizza. The pizza didn't say if it was New York or Chicago, but either way it was flat, greasy and hardly any toppings.

We are on our way to pick up in Pennsylvania, going to Utah.

Love and miss you all

A Little Science Lesson

The weather has been nice, maybe even a little warm for me. Not as hot as a week ago. I thought I was going to die. The humidity was crazy. Sorry, but this is going to be a boring read, ok more boring than usual. This has been a pretty uneventful trip. No bad weather, no traffic situations.

We already have our reload. We pick up in West Virginia going to El Paso. We are going to be out of hours there so it's a good time to get the truck air conditioner fixed, before I die. I'm not excited about staying in El Paso..

In Utah we drove by a site called "The Devil's Slide." A really neat looking site. Here is what I gleaned from the web site.

The sides of the slide are hard, weather-resistant

limestone layers about 40 feet high, 25 feet apart, and several hundred feet in length. In between these two hard layers is a shay limestone that is slightly different in composition from the outer limestone layers. This middle layer is softer, which makes it more susceptible to weathering and erosion, thus forming the chute, or the slide.

While driving through Wyoming we passed a local landmark. A tree growing out of a rock. I think it's

the only tree in the State. The little story is interesting. When the railroad was coming into town they saw this tree growing in a big boulder and they re-routed the tracks so they would not have to move the tree. Once the railroad was done, they would make regular stops so they could water the tree.

In Buford WY there is only one person living in the town. Population 1, it says on the sign. In its hay day, they had 2000 workers. They had a bank and a post office everything a town needs. They were even robbed once by Butch Cassidy.

Another trip through Utah and no Donny Osmond sighting to report. I can tell you other people that I have not seen. I did not see Drew Carey in Cleveland, Ohio. He might be in LA doing the Price is Right. I did not see the "WKRP in Cincinnati" tower. (You kiddos will have to Google that) I have never seen Bruce Springsteen in New Jersey.

We showed up at DuPont in West Virginia to pick up our load to El Paso. It took 8 hours to load, it was heavier than listed in our pretrip information, and it took 3 trips to the nearest scale which is 14 miles one way. Each time we returned to DuPont from the scale, we have to wait in line for them to adjust the load, just so we can go back to the scale and pay another $10 to weigh. About 11 hours after we arrived we have a legal load and are ready to roll. I was sending message after message about needing detention pay, ($30 an hour after the first 2 hours pass). I also let them know we needed the extra miles back and forth to the scale added.

~ 48 ~

This is really a thorn in Will's side. DuPont has a scale on site. It is a huge facility, several square blocks; it's practically the whole town. They have their own street. You get to DuPont, by taking the DuPont Road exit off the freeway. They receive bulk and raw products that need to be weighed coming in. Why don't they let us scale out bound loads? White Trucking said we will not get detention pay because we don't qualify for it! I told them we were scheduled to pick up a load at XX time. The load was not legal for us to drive until 11 hours after our appointment time. What part does not qualify? They never answered. It just took a large portion of good driving time away from my log. Will ran out of hours last night waiting to be loaded. Frustrating, since he was awake and was supposed to be sleeping but of course he couldn't sleep, there was the off chance we could be loaded.

Now we have to re-count our (my) available log hours to see if we can make it to El Paso, since I didn't take any miles off the trip and my day is half over already. As a truck driver we are only allowed to work 14 hours a day. We can only drive 11 hours during the 14 hours. White Trucking is a little confused about us possible not making it on time. They told us we should not have accepted this load if we did not have the hours to run it. Of course I sent a long, detailed message explaining that we did have time to run the load. If it was ready on time, if it weighed what was listed on our pre-plan. If we don't make it to customer on time, that is on them, not us.

We did learn an important science lesson today boys and girls. When the air conditioner in your truck is broke, plus the outside temperature is 104', multiplied by the humidity (oh my gosh have I mentioned the humidity) add the temperature of the floor board inside the truck, least 150 degrees. Plus one soda can left in our drink basket and divided by pi what does that equal? It equals a 7up can bursting out of the pop top, and squirting everywhere.

Oh and an extra FYI you should never have a trailer full of potato chip bags and drive over 7000 in altitude one or two might explode

Love and miss you all

A Wrong Turn? Really?

Another science lesson, two in one trip. There will be bonus points awarded later so pay attention. What happens when you have bald tires on the trailer, a black asphalt road with a temperature above 101? That's right a blowout. We tried to call road service but we were on hold for 15 hot minutes. So Will put air in the tire next to the one that blew, and that got us down the road to the closest truck stop. They did not have a repair shop. They had to send a truck out. The whole thing took almost 3 hours.

We got our air conditioner fixed in El Paso. The international dealer had to replace the high pressure line and the air conditioner compressor... yadda, yadda, yadda, life is good again.

El Paso, Texas was certainly interesting. The driving is almost a free for all. It seemed like you put your blinker on to change lanes and all the cars behind you suddenly decide the lane you want, is also the lane they want, and they don't use blinkers. One of the truckers was saying some people file false hit and run reports against truck drivers. They have 364 days to file after the incident and they usual wait until the deadline nears, then the truck driver can't remember back a year and the company usually settles. The car driver makes notes of what dents etc. the truck or trailer had then just makes sure

it can match up with their car and they also get date and time of where you were, and all that can be confirmed by the Qualcomm satellite in the truck. So the truck driver really has no way to defend himself.

Leaving El Paso on our way to New Mexico, we could see across to Mexico. You could see the fence, and some water. It was the Rio Grande, but looked more like a ditch or a canal, not very grand. The U.S side is at the bottom of the picture. The city of Juarez in the state of Chihuahua, Mexico is the city across from El Paso, Texas.

Will made one interesting observation. Standing on one corner is a Mexican selling a newspaper and on the opposite corner is a white guy with just his hand out and a sign. Not even willing to sell newspapers. We don't know if the Mexican was legal, illegal, homeless or what. But at least he was doing something. And by the way, I'm sure El Paso is Latin for city of used car lots. I have never seen so many car lots.

We delivered in Whittier, California. Then had to drive to Mira Loma and pick up our next load, going to Dallas. We get the load early, that's always good because for some reason White Trucking usually schedules loads to be ready at rush hour. We hook up and hit the road a couple of hours early. Yeah! That means Will can sleep a little bit longer before he has to get up and drive.

Oh but not so fast. The Rand McNally gps is sending me to Dallas one way, the Copilot gps thought a different way was fastest, and White Trucking thinks they know the best route. I had all the directions telling me which freeway to get on, but they didn't tell me how to get to the freeway from where I was sitting. So with minimal yelling and swearing, Will pointed me in the right direction.

I got on CA60 East, then I get on I 215 South, then back on CA60 East. It sounded easy and even looked easy on paper. How could I mess this up? After all it is just reverse of how I got here. With all the confidence in the world, I was off like a heard of turtles.

I turned off the Rand McNally gps, we named her wrong way Randy, because she is always telling us we are over weight limit and not allowed on CA60. Then she spends the rest of the trying to turn us around at every exit. I did get on I 215 south just fine. This is the way we came in, but east and south looked different than west and north but I drove on.

Drive, drive, drive, still no CA60. But I  notice I am now on I 15south, when did that happen? I am one confused little turtle. Oh crap, I need to find something going east. I'd better do it soon before I have to poke the bear again. But there is nothing, no roads going east, how can I get so lost. I know I was looking. How can I keep missing my turns? I just don't know what I keep doing wrong. I wasn't texting. I wasn't putting on make-up. I wasn't shaving my legs.

Oh crap did that sign say San Diego? OK let me think. Think, think, think. San Diego **IS** south of Mira Loma. But it is way, WAY south. There it is again, San Diego. Crap. (I should call my brother, he lives here, and he can tell me where I need to go) Ok, now I really have to do something. I need to stop crying, I need to find an exit that lets me off of I 15 South, and has an immediate entrance to I 15 North. I need to head back to the scene of the crime. Even my fix it plan fell apart. I took an exit that goes directly into a big shopping mall. Who could have guessed I was going to screw that up. Now I have to wake up Will.

Yes, I obviously lived long enough to write this. Will figured out that now it was closer to stay on I 15 South. (which I had just gotten off and parked in a Mall, pissing off shoppers) and head towards I 8 East, than it would be for me to turn around and go back, and start over. After about 372 miles, that would take me to I 10 East, which is where I would have ended up if I followed the original directions.

I cannot figure it out. Where did it all go south, ha ha, no pun intended. Did I learn nothing from the last time I drove so far out of the way? The whole adventure took about 1 1/2 hours and 100 miles out of the way. Luckily there is about 6 extra hours on this load, plenty of time for one more un-planned, site seeing trip.

And so the legend continues. I still cannot find west while looking directly into the setting sun. And even though English is my first and only language, the concept of directional English escapes me.

I don't know how much more of this Will can take. If there comes a point in the future when you can't get ahold of me, or I don't post any blogs, just start looking  for me. But not on our assigned route, look off the route because I'm sure I missed a turn and that was probably the last straw. As soon as I got into Arizona our air conditioner quit, again. Life sucks. We change drivers in Gila, Bend Arizona, 113 degrees btw.

 Will fixes the air conditioner. Life is good. Well as good as it gets today any way.

Love and miss you all sooooooo much

Sometimes, Drivers Can Be Nice

It was my first real driving experience on ice. I have driven on snow, a little bit of ice, but this was an ice storm. I'm going down Shasta and surprised CHP(California Highway Patrol), has not put up chain requirements. Sometimes it seems like they make you chain up at the first sight of a flake. I am also surprised how nice some other truck drivers are. When the going gets tough they get nice and soothing and comforting. One driver came on the CB and asked, "How's it going up there White?" Will picked up the mic and said, "She's doing fine, first big test on ice, and we've got paper rolls."

The other driver said I was doing fine, slow and steady wins the race.

I was driving very slowly, and other drivers would ask if they could come around me. I thought that was weird at first. What do I care if someone passes me, they do all the time. But today they were being nice about it. Instead of saying, "White, move that piece of shit out of my way", they are saying, "White, how's it look up there?" Will would get on the CB and tell them it looks clear, around the next corner there's a free lane you can come around us there. The entire trip down the hill, drivers were getting on the CB giving tips. "There's a tow truck in the center", "Four wheeler in south bound hammer lane, putting on chains", "Four wheeler upside down in number 1 lane", "Hey White Trucking, around the next corner you have a flatbed spun out in your lane". So I start to stop and Will says "What the hell are you doing?" I said slowing down, getting ready to stop because there is a flatbed in my lane up ahead. He said "You're not stopping! You can't stop on an icy hill, just slow down, change lanes." So I slowed down and start to change lanes. The car behind me thought I was going too slow and tried to pass me on my right, as soon as he saw the flatbed he slammed on his brakes, skidded across the road, clipped the left corner of the flatbed, did a 360, slid in front of me, for a split second I was looking at the driver through his wind shield, and finally he came to a stop in the medium. IDIOT!

A little while later a tanker called me on the CB to let me know he was coming around. I said ok looks like you have a clear shot. (Cause that's what I heard Will say). When he got in front of me he told me he was empty. Will got on the CB and said "10-4 we're loaded with paper rolls" I asked Will why I care if he's empty or loaded and why did he keep telling people what we had. Will said empty or loaded makes a big difference in stopping time etc. —

~ 56 ~

DUH I knew that but never thought to tell someone else.

       We made it down the hill, now it's just raining, not freezing rain. Now Will can go back to sleep. He was only sitting up front to help me, and believe it or not he was very calm and helpful.
 Drive careful out there.

Love and miss you all.

A New Grandson

Welcome to the world Robert Jacob, 8lb 15oz.
Mom and dad are doing fine. Jacob joins Mariah
and Kenny. I haven't even met my new
grandson Jake and I miss him already.

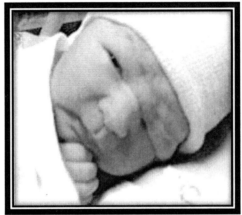

Love and miss you all

POETRY CORNER

There once was a team from
White

Who wished their reloads
came quick

The delay

Affected their pay

In fact the gross made them
quite sick

I sent this to our driver manager. No response
yet.
Love and miss you all

Not a good week

So far this is not starting off to be a good week. We took our time off in Salt Lake City but we were available at 4am. By 8am we still didn't have a load so after eating breakfast ,we head to the White Trucking yard to find an empty trailer. They sent us a load around 9:30 am, headed to Wisconsin. And you guessed it, the load was ready to be picked up the day before. They could have sent it to us at 4am when we were empty and ready for a load. We accepted the load just happy to be rolling.

After a while, Will had time to figure out they were screwing us out 165 miles. We are used to getting taken for about 50 miles per trip. I told Will to tell them to fix the miles or we drop the trailer. He did and when an hour passed with no response I said we need to drop this trailer somewhere, ask them where they want it, (she says with a grin). Will said "And then do what? Sit and not make any money?" I said then why did you threaten them with something you have no intention of carrying through with….just drive.

We finally get to Malt O' Meal and deliver the load. Boy, were they happy to see it. They needed it yesterday. I said they just sent it to us 9 hours ago. They even pulled a trailer off a dock so we could back into it. Then I asked the clerk where do I get an empty? She said they don't have any empty's, they are all assigned outgoing loads. Ok, I'll just wait till this one is unloaded and take it. She said no it's already spoken for. How can that be I just got here, she smiled and said it just is. Well now this really sucks. We already have a reload at Ashley Furniture but can't go without an empty trailer. I message White Trucking that I need an empty. Thirty minutes pass, no response.

"I need an empty trailer or can we bobtail to next customer?"
One hour passes, no response. So I message, "I'm sorry our driver manager is gone today but we still have work to do. I need an empty trailer. Please it has been 1 ½ hours now" "Please sir, may I have another, empty trailer"

"Pretty please with sugar on top, it has now been 2 hours waiting for a response. We still need an empty trailer".

Then a White Trucking truck comes in and drops an empty trailer. So as soon as he left I went over and hooked to it and hot footed it out of the Malt O Meal yard, before they saw me take it. I sent a message telling them I had an empty and what the trailer number was and please send us our next dispatch information. First they told me the trailer was still hooked to the other truck. I told them I am under it and it is following me to Ashley Furniture.

We get to the next customer for a 39,000 pound load and the clerk says they do not have a scale we can use. More and more companies are doing that. We are hauling their freight, yet they make us go out of our way and pay for a scale. They have one on site, they just won't let us use it. The closest scale to Arcadia, Wisconsin is 35 miles away. That would be 70 miles round trip if we had to return to have them adjust the load. Will said if the load was too heavy for us he was just going to leave it at the truck stop.

I said like you left the last load. Well it wasn't too heavy and we took it to Ecru, Mississippi. The gate guard told me they don't have any empty's, they are all being loaded this weekend. I gave him the same speech I gave Malt O' Meal but they have same ears. "Sorry can't give you an empty". Don't they get the give and take of the system? I give you a loaded trailer, you give me an empty trailer. Stop hoarding trailers. They are not even your trailers. The big problem is that our property, the trailer, is on their property, and they have the final word on what comes in and what goes out their gate. There is no way they are lifting the exit gate if you're trying to take a trailer and they said no. Another part of the problem is company's use trailers as storage containers. It's free. It's cheaper than building a new building. Some trucking company's charge shippers a fee for holding and using their trailers, a storage fee. Either White Trucking doesn't charge or they don't charge enough.

      White Trucking sent us a load last night, only 580 miles, so Will denied it. Then again this morning they sent the same load so I denied it. I messaged that this is a team truck and we need team miles. They messaged back and said "Well 580 miles isn't bad for a weekend". WHAT!! I said "I can't believe you really think that waiting 11 hours to pick up a load going 580 miles to a city where we typically sit for a day is a good load for a team. If that is true then send me home White Trucking does not need team drivers. Each driver is capable of driving about 600 miles so that, my dear, makes it a solo load."

When Will woke up he tells me I should have taken that load. Now he's mad because we are sitting. I said don't get all pissy with me for turning down the same load you turned down last night. If you want to make every decision, every time then fine, I will wake you up every time the direction on the gps doesn't match the directions from White Trucking. Every time I need to clarify is east the same as south on this route. You might as well take the qualcom back to the sleeper so you can reply to every message. He said that that would be fine it would save us time and unnecessary miles when I get lost. I'll never retire at this rate. I need to buy more lottery tickets and do better at the casinos. Maybe I should get life insurance on Will. I'm going to kill him, either by getting lost one too many times or never mind forget I said anything.

To top off a fun filled time in Ecru, Mississippi, while we were parked another truck hit us. We had the curtain closed I was in bed and Will was watching TV, since he was wide awake expecting to be driving. Then I hear a crunching sound and Will swearing and the truck door open. As soon as it happened about a dozen drivers came running over. "I saw the whole thing, that trainer was not doing his job, he set that driver up wrong, he was never going to be able to make that swing.' Anyway Will was looking at the truck and I went and talked to the trainer and he said we should just call the police and let them do the paper work. I said ok and went into the truck stop and asked them to call. They said the police are already on the way. When I got back to the truck, sure enough there were 3 patrol cars. Wow what service, or maybe a slow night in Ecru, or maybe this has happened before and they know the appropriate show of force. Will said the trainer went into the truck and stayed there until the police showed up. We figured neither him nor the driver wanted to take their chances with a dozen of bubba truckers. At any rate not much damage. We

need to replace the right fender mount mirror, fix some cracked fiberglass and have them look at the head light. It's cracked but still works. After calming down we both felt sorry for the trainee. He seemed like a decent guy, just a bummer now he has an accident on his record and he's just starting.

The good news is we will be home for Easter. Our newest grandson is being baptized Easter Sunday. I can keep myself busy and away from Will by planning a big dinner.

Love and miss you all

Graceland, Graceland, Memphis Tennessee

Is it wrong that I was singing Paul Simon's Graceland rather than an Elvis song, while touring Graceland?

I apologize in advance. I left my camera at the hotel and only had my cell phone. I don't have a smart phone and the camera options are not that good so they are kind of small pictures.

Note: It turned out I could not use the pictures I took of Graceland because the resolution was not good enough to print, even though they look great on line. I did include these pictures on my blog site. Sorry

It was amazing. Mostly for the fact that it was not at all what I was expecting. It is not a big secluded mansion. I have seen bigger built in pools, well everywhere. The entire house sits on about 13 acres. The house is only 10 miles from downtown, not secluded; you can see it from the street. The information says the sqft is about 10,000 but that seems like a lot. I wonder if that includes the out buildings. He bought the property in 1957 for $90,000! Can you believe it? Part of the sales agreement was to keep the name Graceland, it was named for the original owner Grace Toff. Elivs said he liked the name so that was not a deal breaker.

We were not allowed up stairs to the private residence area. The bedrooms and of course the bathroom where he died were off limits. But the majority of the house looked like a normal 60's-70's home. There are only 5 bedrooms in the house.

The kitchen is normal size, maybe even small. The Kitchen I grew up in was larger than this kitchen. The furniture in the living room was white so was the carpet. Off the living room is the music room with a black baby grand piano, the entrance to the music room was an archway with 2 stained glass panels of peacocks. It is also where his casket was placed for his funeral. The dining room has a table that seats 6, white carpet and blue suede curtains. The den or rather, the jungle room was a sunken room. It was cool looking but I can't say I could imagine orgy's going on there. The carpet was green shag. The ceiling was also carpeted, they said as a sound buffer from the music. The furniture was dark wood, mostly hand crafted exotic woods. A nice, African motif. A big burro coffee table, like the one my dad made. The coolest feature was an entire brick wall waterfall. There were stuffed animals that the tour guide said belonged to Lisa Marie. BTW Elvis only called his daughter Lisa Marie, never just Lisa.

The billiard room is different, cool, but different. The same material covers the walls, furniture and ceiling. 400 yards of material. It took 3 workers 10 days to finish the project. There is a rip in the felt on the pool table and sorry I forgot who ripped it, but at the time I was impressed.

After we leave the house you walk to the trophy room, actually trophy building. A big, 2 story room. It has his gold records, some of his touring jumpsuits and pictures. Really, a neat place. Big screen TV's playing his concerts and interviews. His movie memorabilia is not there, it is in a separate building across the street. Don't worry one price gets you into everything.

The last thing you visit outside is the meditation garden, near the built in pool. Buried there are Elvis, his mother, his father, and his grandmother. Strangely enough, when Elvis had his mother's remains moved from Tupelo to Graceland he chooses not to include his twin's remains. I thought that was odd. Throughout the tour you can see how much he loved his mother; there are pictures of her everywhere.

Across the street are several more sights. His two planes. One is called the Lisa Marie, the other is Hound Dog. You can walk through both planes. That was cool.

There are two buildings one with just his cars. Yes you can see his pink Cadillac and his motorcycles. Another building has just his movie stuff. Posters, hand written notes on scripts, they have out takes playing on some of the TV's. You can watch an Elvis movie in booths that look like 1950's cars. There are about 25 cars there. Elvis drove all of them at one time or another.

It was such a cool place. Really a place everyone should see. I like Elvis, but never considered myself an Elvis fanatic. But his life history is so interesting. Humble beginnings, rise to stardom, and finally his fall from grace. I'm glad I finally talked Will into doing something on our time off.

His mother and sister are real Elvis Fan's. Have all his movies and records. We were able to get some good pictures and souvenirs for them. Would I go again, probably not but I'm glad I can say I went. I think anyone that likes music should go. It's music history in our own back yard.

Love and miss you all,

Thank you, thank you very much.

Home time was great, always too short

        I am thankful we made it home for our oldest daughter's graduation. She is the first one in the family to graduate college. We are the very proud parents of a dual degree daughter. Legal secretary and administrative assistant. She did not begin college until she was married with children, which made it more difficult for her and makes her accomplishment that much sweeter. Congratulations Paige

        We went to the zoo. They were having a dinosaur exhibit. My grandson was so excited. He called me weeks before to tell me all about what we were going to see. When am I going to be home? Making sure I don't miss our date. "We have to go before they are gone, Grandma!"

        The day we went to the zoo, it was the hottest day of the year. Kenny did not want to see anything else. He wanted to go straight to the Dino-exhibit. But the younger kids wanted to see everything. Finally the big moment has arrived we are in line to buy tickets to the dinosaur exhibit. They had loud speakers throughout the zoo so you could hear the fierce roar of the enormous animals. We walk up to the first dinosaur. I was so excited and told Kenny, "There it is, stand close so I can get a picture". His response was, "Why it's not real, wait to we get to the real ones. Come on lets hurry grandma".

        My heart was broken when I saw the look on his face and explained to him that there were no real dinosaurs anymore. I said honey you know dinosaurs are extinct. He thought it was going to be like Jurassic Park.

He asked "Then why do they have fake dinosaurs at the zoo? The zoo is for alive animals". After seeing the disappointment on his face I wondered the same thing. He was miserable the rest of the day. I felt so sorry for him.

The Baptism was beautiful. Every time I come home I'm remind what we are working towards, permanent home time.

The rest of home time was great, but I will never forget that trip to the zoo.

Love and miss you all.

A lesson Learned

We are sitting in a truck stop and after getting fuel, a truck pulls forward, parks and goes into the store with his shower bag.

The truck started to roll backwards. The driver parked next to him jumped out, yelled at the other driver, but he did not hear him. So he yanked the air-lines off. The lack of air automatically sets the brakes. To add insult to injury, the driver reached under and pulled the 5th wheel latch. Now the trailer is no longer attached to the tractor. When the driver of the truck comes back from his shower, he will see his truck about 20 feet from where he parked it and no air lines attached. He might figure out what happened, reattach his air lines and start to leave in a hurry before he catches hell from other drivers about his stupidity. But since the other driver pulled the 5th wheel latch, the trailer will drop to the ground when it is no longer supported by the tractor.

I bet that driver never forgets to set his brakes again. Sorry we won't be able to stick around and watch the show. Our driver change is over, time to hit the road.
Love and miss you all.

What is up with all the mosquitos?

Will drives with the windows down. But that lets in mosquitos. Now I look like I have chicken pox. I'm sure I will contract Dengue Fever or Malaria.

For years Will has been making fun of me for always putting on bug spray. He tells me to stop complaining about the heat and drive with the windows down. I told him mosquitos will eat me alive, not to mention the other bugs. Now he is being helpful. He bought me some itch medicine, and driving with the windows

up. Now he says we will have to get the air conditioner fixed, again.

Love and miss you all

Is there a special group for people like me?

Some university must be doing a study. I cannot be the only one who is afflicted with the directional comprehension disorder. It can't be a rare disease or there would be no GPS industry.

We were taking a load from Waco, Texas to Corrine, Utah. I was set up by the gps at the beginning of my route to the shipper. I went in circles twice through one of the roundabouts that are everywhere now, and so convenient for a semi-truck to drive through. Finally, through trial and error, I figured out she wanted me to take the third right exit through the roundabout. We are loaded with great value baby diapers headed for Wal-Mart warehouse in Utah. I was doing ok. We were tight for time on this load we have just enough hours between us to get there and since we have worked our 70 hours this week it will be time for our 34 hours off.

Ok everybody take out your map and follow along, try to see where Leslie went wrong

I'm on US **287N**.
My next turn is US**281N** then I**44E** in Wichita Falls TX.
Ok no problem. As luck would have it **281N** and I**44E** are the same road.
My next turn is back onto **287N** in Amarillo. So I'm driving and driving next thing I see is a welcome to Oklahoma sign.
CRAP how did this happen. I need to turn around now before I get way lost. Too late for that, I'm on the Oklahoma turn pike. There's no getting off at the next exit, going over the over pass and back on in the opposite direction on a turn pike. So I try to quietly pay my toll. Don't want to poke the bear if I don't have too. The Bear Whisper can only do so much.
Oh good a rest stop and it is in the center so both directions can use it. I'll just go in the East bound side and drive around and exit on the West bound side. I've done it before on the Kansas turnpike. Can't pull it off in Oklahoma. There is a Jersey barrier separating the east and west side. Ok back on the **44E** turn pike. But even I know that Utah is not east of Oklahoma, which I'm not even supposed to be

there in the first place. Well there's no place to get off so I just have to drive and pray.

Please God do not let Will wake up, place him in a coma until I work this out.

Eventually (and I use that term loosely, more like 190 miles later) I end up in Lawton Oklahoma. I get off the turn pike. My plan was to get right back on and head back to the scene of the crime.

At warp speed of course. (190 miles x2) But the GPS told me to head west on 62. Well, west is the general direction I need to go, and according to its directions I'm only 109 miles from us287.

Yes, new plan. Please God 109 miles is only an hour and a half. That's all the more time I need.

But I need to take care of the GPS, that loud mouth, tattle tale B-itoch. I turn her volume all the way down. But there are more flaws in my survival plan. Who put all these stinkin' little towns on route 62? I need to stay at 65mph. I can't be slowing down and stopping for lights, school buses and pedestrians. That might wake the bear, let him hibernate.

It's 2 o'clock I normally change the radio to Wolf Blitzer. If I turn it on Will might hear it and get up I usually am done driving around 5. So I decide not to turn on CNN and put on the classic radio, Jack Benny show. Yeah, yeah, good plan.

Only 59 miles to go. Less than an hour. 30 miles, I might just live long enough to get treatment.

The sleeper light comes on.

Oh come on are you kidding me, since I wasn't struck by lightning I thought we had a deal.

Crap another flaw.

Why does Oklahoma have road signs that say Oklahoma? Why do the towns have to have Oklahoma on the city sign, don't these people know they live in a city that is in the State of Oklahoma already. Do they have to be reminded of what state they live in? How depressing to be reminded every moment of every day that you live in Oklahoma. Texas doesn't torture residents like that.

Don't open the curtain.....Don't open the curtain...

Wait, I can see a way out of this, only 20 miles and I'm back in Texas.

YES!!! I made it to Texas. (Words I never thought I'd say) So now if he looks out at least he will see Texas road signs etc. Cross off number 118 out of 500 things that must happen to get through this. Now I am only 8 miles from being back on US287.

Will says where are we?

Almost to 287, (what, I didn't lie)

What are you doing on 62?

(How did he know that??) I missed my turn and had to get on this to get back to 287 which is only 5 miles away. (Again, not a lie)

Hum?

Did he buy it? Can you hear someone having a stroke? Do I look suspicious, while trying not to look guilty?

Crap, another flaw in my survival plan. The laptop! Why didn't I spill lemon aid on it? Mental note for next time, no wait, no next time.

Now he has it up and is looking at it. Then he closes the curtain
Ok God, I owe you one, Thanks.

100 miles? You missed your turn 100 F'ing miles ago? Why didn't you stop at around 50 F'ing miles ago?

Only 100 miles, boy I'd fess up to being JUST 100 miles off.

I said cant you be glad that I figured it out without waking you up?
He must have known not to start with me. Because that's as far as it went.

Now we are really tight for time on this load. We have 1068 more miles. We started the day with 1309 miles to go. I drove all day and got nowhere and I can only drive 6 hours and 45 min tomorrow. We change drivers at the Flying J in Amarillo. Will was still mad and goes in first. I grab my wallet and walk into the Denny's beside the Flying J by accident, but I didn't tell Will that.

I really love and miss you all

Family

Because of our soon to be, but not soon enough, ex son in law, our daughter needed to pack and move her stuff with short notice. My family dropped what they were doing and everyone showed up to help.

Everyone except her mother and father were there to help. I hate this job. I don't like not being there when I'm needed. I hate being gone all the time. I hate that she has to go through this on her own. Will told me to stop crying over it. I should be thankful for what I have. I guess he's right. So maybe I'm crying because I have the best family anyone could hope for. Maybe she isn't going through this on her own. Maybe I'm more blessed than I know.

I love and miss you all so much.

Back up in Redding California

Well its Friday, wish I could say TGIF. This is only our second load of the week. (No $$)

It started ok. We picked up paper rolls in Springfield, after our 2 days at home. Drove down to Fresno where this load was t-called so we could pick up FedEx Wednesday at 4am. Wednesday we go to pick up our FedEx. Get there at 2:00 am, the load is ready at 4am, they give us the paper work. While Will is hooking up to the trailer I'm calling the HazMat hotline to report we will be carrying HazMat, (extra $$). Then before we are done, FedEx comes up to us and tells us the load was cancelled. After some frantic phone calls and messages to who-ever-cares, on the qualcomm, it was confirmed the load was cancelled. When I asked about a new load I was told, Sorry, contact your DM for a new dispatch.

I said last time a FedEx load was cancelled from SeaTac to Oakland we were told to run the empty trailer. We were told not this time. So we waited. Our DM comes in at 6am. That's funny, I thought trucking was a 24/7 job. No load. 7am no load. 8 am ah yes a load. 4 hours after our load was canceled. They send us a load to be picked up in Antioch, CA and going to Toppenish, WA. It is sheets of tin for making cans. This load was for Trader Joes. Next time you buy something in a can there think of us.

The weather was just awful in California. And with the sideways rain and wind by the time we got to the shipper in Antioch, our dry trailer was rejected because it was filled with water. Some patch work they had done to fix some holes, failed. We had to go towards Travis Air force Base and get another trailer at the Clorox plant. This time the rain was more normal and the trailer stayed dry and we were loaded. We were loaded at 5pm in the Bay Area! Just another good omen for this trip.

We were able to drive from Antioch to Redding before the weather shut us down for the night. Snow, ice and Wind. CHP closed the road. We parked on the side of the road with all the other trucks because there was no room at the truck stop. The bad weather was not exactly where we were. The dangerous road conditions were about 20 miles north of us. It's one thing to be shut down with snow and ice all around you. It's frustrating to be shut down due to bad weather you can see.

We hit the road again at 5:45 am. Got on the freeway and stopped. I drove a total of 3.2 miles before we had to stop. There were two lanes of trucks. Also the ramps were full. The school buses couldn't get the kids to school because they couldn't get on the freeway. The residents of Redding couldn't get to work because of the backup. The traffic jam went from Dunsmuir to Anderson. News stations said the backup was 25 miles!!

We sat there for about 4 hours before moving—YES! Ok buckle up here we go-- nope here we stop 200 feet north of where we just were. Take off the seat belt, pick up my book The Stupidest Angel by Christopher Moore funny, funny, funny. If you need a laugh and like a slightly twisted humor this is for you. A Christmas story without all the Christmas stuff.

Fruit bats, zombies, sword swinging warriors, an accidental murder of Santa, and a little boy's wish that starts the whole thing rolling.

We inch along the freeway every so often, and now we are going down to 2 lanes. Trucks in right lane of course. So now the backup is unbelievable. South bound traffic was moving along just fine. Which was even more frustrating. Someone from the south bound lane came on the CB and said, "Hey north bounders, don't worry, you'll get through this. It's ok. This too shall pass". His encouragement was NOT received well.

Another hour passes, the weather has cleared, no rain and sunny. We hear on the CB that they are opening the left lane to trucks and taking down the chain inspection and the chain requirements. Ok, now we are really rolling, clipping along at a speed usually reserved for speeding Segway's. I must tell you it was quite a site seeing nothing but two lanes of trucks in front of me and two lanes behind. People were standing on the overpasses, taking pictures. I got out and took a couple of pictures.

A chain check area is something the Department of Transportation set's up just for truckers. For miles in advance you see signs telling you to carry chains. Different states have different requirements. California has 3 different levels of chain requirements. You must carry chains in Colorado between Sept 1 and May 31. Oregon and Washington allow you to have a drag chain on your trailer. And so on. According to California law we are currently required to carry chains in the pass areas.

So why do they pull every single truck over on the side of the road, jump up on your running boards and ask, "Driver, do you have your chains?"

Yes, of course it's the law. Besides can't you see them, they are the jingly things hanging on the side of the truck. It is also the law that I have a valid commercial driver's license with a haz-mat endorsement so I can deliver this load safely, but you didn't ask that. Why did you waste my time to ask a question you can answer yourself by looking at my chains? That's what I wanted to say. In reality I simply 'Yes sir'. They don't ask the cars if they have chains, and a large majority of the weather related accidents are from cars.

From Trucking Global News:
Research says nearly 75 percent of all crashes involving semis are unintentionally caused by the person driving the passenger vehicle. And in 35 percent of those the car was in one of the trucks four blind spots.

Once we started rolling someone came on the CB and said "Ok drivers, let's just keep the wheels turning, if everyone can keep their testosterone in check and nobody F@*$'s up we won't be stuck behind an accident".

We get up the hill and the weather is beautiful.

We delivered on time, at 9pm, and as I write this it is now 9am, and no load. 12 hours. I don't believe it. Trucking is a 24/7 business except for White Trucking. It is an 8 to 5 Monday thru Friday business.

Our diver manager keeps telling us that freight is down. The freight gods are just not with us today. Can't wait to see what happens next. What an interesting ride this has been.

Love and miss you all

Trailer stocking and bad weather.

Why are we constantly looking for a stinking empty trailer? They'll send us to Stockton, telling us sears has one. Send us to Patterson, Khols has three. Don't take any from Costco.

One time we could not find an empty everywhere they sent us. So they said they had a driver that was sitting over in the Lathrop yard with an empty and he would hold it for us. Ok so over there we go, he's gone but we got the trailer and went to hook up to it and the lights didn't work, and no shop to fix it, luckily we found another empty there. Not just a bulb that Will can fix.

The last time we found an empty with a flat. We tried to get the shop to fix it and 2 hours later he still never got around to it. So we left without an empty. I told Will we should have hooked up to it, drove down the block, then called   for road service. He didn't think that would work. How do you know if you don't try? It's not just us. Every time we drop at the Lathrup yard there is a line of drivers at the window asking for empty trailer locations.

One time I thought Will was going to have a stroke. He's there at the window with   several other drivers asking for empties and one of the local drivers, the guy that works 8-5, says, "Oh you need empties? I made three deliveries today I guess I should have brought back empty's with me. But I wanted something to do later today".

OMG, I could hear the vein in his neck start throbbing. He just shook his head and left. Two other drivers threw up their hands and left. One driver actually voiced his opinion about the local driver out loud. He must be new here.

It's funny how men and women see the same thing and associate it a different way. For instance, we are delivering our FedEx load in Kent, Washington. We don't have a reload, its 11:30 pm and we are looking for a place to park for the night. We turn the corner and there are two buildings. Barely lit by street lamps. One big blue with yellow letters and right across the street is a smaller building, same shade of blue with yellow letters. I say, "That's weird, I

 wonder why they have two Ikea stores across from each other" Will says "Ikea? I was thinking that was the biggest Napa I've ever seen"[1] Ikea was the big

building, Napa was the little one.

I did grab a couple of books last time I was home. How the Irish saved

civilization. The untold story of history between the fall of Rome and the raise of medieval Europe and In my own words, the autobiography of the Dalai Lama. Will really needs to read that one. He is just so intense about things. Everything is like the last straw. We have to hurry there is no time on this load. We don't want to get stuck in rush hour traffic. Hurry up go around this guy before we get to the hill. Hurry, the sooner we get there the sooner I can get some sleep. And on and on. He is always so pessimistic about things. I told him a glass half full, will still quench your thirst. He says wtf does that mean. I keep telling him I can't afford to keep giving him my karma points. 'Earn your own' that attitude probably cost me some points

Our trip from Grandview, Washington, to Fresno, CA was anything but uneventful.

We picked up our loaded trailer from Wal-Mart and headed out. The route they sent us included WA22 to US97. It didn't take long for snow to start covering the already frozen roads. We turned on to WA22 only a few miles on that road and it quickly became white out conditions. Huge flakes.

So Will, thank goodness he was driving, made an executive decision, to turn around and take I82 to I84.

That plan worked well enough, it got us to Biggs Junction, Oregon where I84 and US97 meet. That is where we stayed the night. We had to hunt for a spot and almost didn't find one. Luckily a truck left his spot and we grabbed it.

Leaving Biggs Junction, Oregon, No one else on the road.

We left Biggs at 7am and made it to Chiloquin at 1:30 only 250 miles.

Slow going. I passed several accidents. It seems like the sand is never on our side of the road.

Now we are sitting 3 miles past the Kla-Mo-Ya casino, we've been waiting in line for about 1 hour so far, because there is an accident about 10 miles in front of us. If we'd know that we would have stayed at the casino and donated some money.

After sitting for about 2 hours, we were again on our way. I am happy to report the rest of the trip WAS UNEVENTFUL.

I have to make a peanut butter sandwich and go to bed. I need to be all rested for our 4am FedEx. I can't help but worry about what will be waiting for us when we get to Kent. More local deliveries? Or nothing at all because it will be Friday. I already know it is hoping for too much to have a south bound load ready and waiting for us. I would much rather take our 34 off down in Lathrup. Then we can be there are available to FedEx Monday.

Love and miss you all,

What? Who Me, Lost?

Just when you thought it was safe for me to drive up and down I5. Here is a

picture of the Blue Angels in Seattle. The only other 2 words that make my heart skip a beat is 'Fleet Week'.

Our driving schedule it pretty laid out. South bound, Will picks up in Seattle drives to PDX then to Redding, California. Then I drive from Redding to LAX. North bound, Will drives from LAX to Hayward. I drive from Hayward (Oakland airport) to Salem, Will drives to PDX, then to Seattle. Then we do it all again. Easy Peasy

Will thinks the way I remember how to get to LAX is too confusing. This is how I do it. I'm on I5, take it to the 405, then exit 45, then exit 5. I wrote it down for him **I5**, **405**, (cross off the zero,) exit **45**, (cross off the 4) exit **5**. The route from Hayward to I5 is just as easy to remember. 880, 80, 505, 5.

I did the route a few times then, feeling a little cocky, decided I can turn off the GPS. I don't need no stinkin' gps, I know where I'm going, this is so easy a monkey could, oh look a balloon.

While on the 80 I saw a bunch of hot air balloons. I was taking pictures thinking this was pretty. When I was done I put the camera down and after driving a while (really folks it was only about 25 miles,  hardly story worthy) I noticed the road was still 4 lanes. Usually by this time I'm on 2 lanes.

With sun flowers on both sides. Ok, I know the drill, turn on the GPS, turn the sound down, take the next exit, cross over, and return to the scene of the crime. The whole adventure cost about 50 miles and close to an hour. So I didn't make it to Salem to change drivers, we changed in Albany. Really I don't know why I'm telling you this.

I do get to run into a friend of mine, that I knew when we both had a normal job. Her and her husband drive for another company and their route is FedEx in Mira Mar to Portland. I ran into her at Wal-Mart last time we were home, (it's a small world) we are usually north bound when they are south. She'll call me to say she just passed me and that there is a fire up ahead but it's on her side so not to worry. Just a fire, no worries, no reason for anyone to stop. It's kind of nice knowing someone else let their husband talk them into doing this crazy job.

We are sitting in hotel in Fontana because our north bound load doesn't pick up till tonight at midnight. And since our air conditioner isn't working 100%. Will can't sit in that truck all day. Although it doesn't matter to him that I sit in the hot truck all day driving. The sleeper air conditioner works fine.

My air conditioner is a complicated system involving a small fan, duct tape

and prayer that the air actually gets to me. They make a window screen for semi-trucks. Apparently a working air conditioner must be a rare thing.

I used to roll the windows down but the other day driving through Willows, CA; something came in the window and hit my neck. At first I thought it was a fly or a bee and I just reached up to grab it and throw it back out the window. But I could feel it. It was huge. It started to move in my fingers. I could feel it wiggling and squirming to get away. It took up my entire hand. I threw it on the floor, along with some of my hair. (I'm honestly peeing a little re-telling the story) I screamed, I quickly, swerved to the side of the road, and stop, mostly, off the road. I pull the air brakes before I came to a full and complete stop.

Will is up and poking his head through the curtain.

"What's wrong, what happened?

I said, from the running boards outside the driver's door, "A bird or a bat or something flew in the window and bit me. It's there on the floor board, KILL IT!" He looks and sees the locust and says,

"You dynamited the brakes for that? You Kill it."

What a Wuss.

And that's why I can't drive with the windows down, no matter how hot it is.
Ok gotta go do laundry.

Love and miss you all

Just Venting

One of the biggest complaints I have is the way we are paid. We get paid by the mile. We do not get paid for every mile we drive. We are paid by a system called the Rand McNally Household Goods mileage. Some drivers get paid a percentage of the load but we do not. We do not get paid address to address. Basically zip code to zip code. On average we are under paid 50-75 miles per trip simply because we are not paid door to door. We do not get paid the extra miles it might take to drive from the customer to a scale then back to the customer to adjust the load. Companies Will has worked for in the past paid Hub Miles. They had a little mileage counter on your front Hub, it was recorded when you started and again when your pay period was over. Very fair. Ah, Good times, Good times. You were paid for every single mile you drove.

We also have to pay an over mileage fee for every mile we drive over 11,000. Just like when you lease a car you are allowed XX amount of miles every month and if you drive over those miles you pay an extra fee. As a team truck we always drive over those miles. I really don't know how a solo owner/op does it.

Another, gotcha, is at the end of the month we are given a fuel rebate. It is a complex math equation, but if we keep our fuel mileage around 7 mpg we get a rebate on the amount of fuel we purchased. That sounds pretty easy and straight forward. Here's the rub, let's say we actually drive 20,000 miles for a month. We are paid for 18,500 dispatched miles. You can see right away the difference between address to address vs. zip code to zip code miles? We will pay an excess mileage fee of .09¢ for every mile over 11,000 per month. We pay that fee for miles driven whether they are dispatched miles or not. We have to pay fuel to drive those extra miles, which we are not paid for. Our fuel rebate is figured first by estimating our fuel mileage for our dispatched miles. Then that is compared to our actual mpg, which, as you can see will included more than our dispatched miles. They may or may not be 'close enough' to warrant a fuel rebate.

I'm not complaining, well ok I might be. We are adults. We read the contract. Will understands the trucking business more than I do so he even understood the contract. Everyone is in the same boat as us. Nobody is picking on us.

I'm just in a bad mood today. It just seems like truck drivers get the short end of the stick. You can't deliver too early or late or you're fined. If the freight is damaged, you're fined. Even though we do not load or package the freight we are responsible for it. Even if we arrive on time for a delivery, if the customer takes their time unloading us; we might run out of hours. The business will not allow us to sit on their property. Even though it is illegal for us to drive once we are out of hours. That has only happened to us once, because we are a team, one of us usually has hours to drive. We were resetting our hours, that time. We were doing a rolling re-start rather than sitting the entire 34 hours. Here's how that works. The first driver,

Will, goes off-duty while I drive for 10 hours. Then both drivers are off duty for 24 hours. The first driver then comes back on-duty while the second driver finishes the remaining 10 hours of the restart period. It minimizes our down time, but I don't like it. They actually unloaded faster than we had planned and I was not able to come up yet. We just had to hang out for 45 min, and then we left. But that could happen more often for a solo driver. The law says we have to have 10 hours off before we can drive. When a solo is out of hours he has no options, he is sitting.

California is the worst. There are so many places where we deliver but we are not allowed to drive. If that makes any since. Even in warehouse areas there are no semi parking signs everywhere. Really what are we supposed to do? I'm glad you asked, we drive around the block until the business opens and we can deliver. Or we sit but one driver has to remain up front. That way when a cop comes by and asks if we saw the no parking sign, we say yes we are just checking our map or calling our dispatcher. And that usually works as long as we move along and are not there when they come back.

If we break down on the side of the road we face a whole new set of problems. We have been lucky and always made it to a rest area or truck stop whenever we had a flat or break down. But you don't always have that choice. If you break down on the side of the road, the police will show up and give you the once over, maybe twice. You will probably get a ticket for equipment failure for whatever caused you to break down. Then they could double check your logs. Did you remember to record your last bathroom stop or did you think it was quick enough that you didn't need to write it down? Did you do your math right, are you sure you haven't driven 15 minutes longer than you are allowed? How's your weight, did you put in too much fuel are you over weight thinking you would burn it off before the next scale house? I know it's day light but, do your head lights work? Are you sure you were driving the speed limit? They <u>will</u> do the math and figure how many miles away you were at your last stop and what time it was recorded, and then figure if you could have arrived at your current location driving the speed limit. If not, you're getting a ticket. And now that you are stopped, did you remember to log that you are stopped?

So next time you are stuck in traffic worried about getting home before your dinner gets cold or you miss your show, think about the line of trucks in the lane next to you. The traffic is costing them money. Fees for being late. The cost of fuel to sit and idle. Remember we only get paid to drive, not to sit. If the delay takes too long we may miss a pick up time and pay a fee or lose the load entirely. And don't forget they are away from their family for weeks and months at a time to make a living. We are just trying to make a living, and get home safe to our family, the same as you.

If you bought it, a truck brought it.

Love and miss you all so much

Texas Is Just Another Southern Place. 'Yall

We delivered our load one day early, no thanks to White Trucking. Every time we asked them if we could deliver early the answer was, your DM is not here. I've started looking for the customers info on line and if I can just give them a call and ask them if we can deliver early without any penalty or fine, I know it's just another way to take money from us, fine you if you're early or late. The customer let us dock and unload. So good, we are available 24 hours before our original plan. I send in a message saying we are empty and ready for our next load. First they were surprised but eventually realized we were telling the truth. It takes a short while, but they give us a fairly short run. Not a solo run but definitely not a team run. It is Hebron KY, to Roanoke TX, 900 miles. Just one and a half shifts, as Will likes to say. Each of us usually drives 600 miles a shift

We drive to Florence, Kentucky.
The water tower says, 'Florence y'all '.

We can't pick up the load until Tuesday, the next day. We are just on the outskirts of Cincinnati, Ohio, and there were

thunder storms all night, and tornado warnings. I couldn't sleep because I have the TV on listening to the local TV station and keeping an ear on the CB. I went into the truck stop to check out their tornado shelter and didn't see one. Where am I supposed to go? Will says to just stay in the truck and calm down. I'm safe in the truck. If you have not seen it, watch this video.

http://www.youtube.com/watch?v=bqhovF-O98Q

When morning comes we get a message that our load canceled. After waiting a while they send us another load. It was worse than the first one. Only 300 miles, from Greenfield, Indiana, to Cookeville, Tennessee.

Big whoop. I asked if this was part of the company's new plan. They just implemented a new expedited team freight division. We were put in that division, division 757 w/ hazmat endorsements. It was over one hour and we can't get any information on the load. We can't just up and drive there because we didn't even get a street address yet, just the pick-up city and delivery city. So we wait and wait, all the while getting more and more frustrated. I let our DM know that so far we have $139 going into our bank account. We are not going to be working just so we can make the truck payments, then White Trucking shorts our loads, they figure WTH, the truck expenses are paid. Well we are going to accept every load they give us and when we can't make a decent wage we will be able to argue we took all you gave us, and it didn't work.

As fate would have it, that load eventually canceled. I sent an open message to Phoenix, the mother ship, telling them how long a team has sat without a load. That I thought we were in division 757, the team division, where are the team loads? We are not just working for the company store. We are not out here on vacation. We have bills to pay. I ask them what we are doing wrong; give us some advice on how we can improve our miles. I knew it wasn't us it was them but thought I would be polite about it. I tell them something has to change if we are going to continue to work here. We either need a new DM or a new terminal or we will look for a new employer

We finally got a load to Maryland, after turning down a load to New York. We cannot drive into New York; we did not purchase the extra permit for that State. Maryland is only 500 miles from here, but from there we pick up a load and head for Tucson, Arizona. Driving through Kentucky I saw a yellow warning sign it said "Fallen rock area" Even the signs have an accent. Out west we say "Falling rock area".

Sometime during the thunderstorm last night, lightning struck a church with a big statue of Jesus. On the morning news they played one of the 911 calls. The caller said "Jesus was on fire! First it was just his hand but now it is all of Jesus." The church said Jesus was insured, but it would take more than 3 days to resurrect this Jesus. I don't know how they kept a straight face during that report.

Night time as fallen in West Virginia, my shift is over and Will is up doing his pretrip and getting his snacks ready for his shift. The fire flies are just starting to come out so I'll watch them for a little while. When the fire fly's hit the windshield, if you turn the wipers on, it smears them and leaves a glowing streak across the glass, but only for a second or two. Maybe sick and twisted, but I'll watch anyway. We don't have fireflies in Oregon.

Then I am off to watch Lost. Our son has been recording and putting them on a DVD for me. I almost forgot to tell you, I got a Kindle! It is so much easier to read at night not having to juggle the book light. Now I have all of the Diana Gabaldon books from her Outland series. I love it. You have got to read it. A time traveling, Scottish Highland, love story. If I was not already married, I would still be looking for my true love for all the ages, my very own Jamie Fraser.

Love and miss you all

Spring Time Sure Brings Out the Animals

This has been a deadly month. Mice, skunks, cats and rabbits running all over the roads. I hit a little bird; they should be able to fly faster than that. I hit a pheasant. I felt bad for that one. He took off from the right side of the road and he almost hit the windshield, but he gained enough height to just hit the sky rise thing. That hit hard. There was a truck passing me at the time and when he went by he just shook his head and said ' He almost made it, normally they can out run a White Trucking truck'. I almost hit a crane, you can see them start flapping their wings faster, as the truck gets closer, I'm telling them faster, faster, and he just pulled his legs in at the last minute. Whew!

There have been skunks every couple of miles. I haven't hit one of them thank goodness. Then there was a turtle, yes a turtle. We were going east and he was trying to cross over to the pond on the west side I don't know how he got over on this side anyway. He just took like two steps, his whole body wasn't even across the white line on the shoulder, I missed him and there was no body right behind me. I know he did not make it. He had all of the east bound side to cross, the grassy medium and then if he still had the energy, the west side to cross. Poor thing. There are armadillos in a lot more states than I thought. I'm surprised Kansas and Missouri have any wild deer left. You can't drive a mile without seeing one on the side of the road. They are smaller than the deer in Oregon. I was surprised that Chicago and New Jersey had deer taking a nap on the side of the road too. That's what we used to tell the girls, there just taking a nap.

I never saw Bruce Springsteen in New Jersey. Will never sees Paris Hilton and he eats at In and Out Burgers every time we are in California. I did see Toby Keith's equipment truck; it was going the opposite direction so I couldn't get a picture. I also saw his I Love This Bar, bar in Oklahoma and I saw his name on the city sign of Moore Ok, 'Proud home of Toby Keith' saw some NASCAR car haulers. Also going the opposite direction, so no pictures.

We should be in Oregon Saturday. Back where the rain is normal rain. And the temperature is a normal temperature.

Love and miss you all

Chain, Chain, Go Away

We bought a set of cable chains a while ago and today we got to use them. They sure were easier to put on, and not to mention considerably lighter. We still have a set of regular chains in case the cable ones didn't work out. Besides you can only use cable chains on certain tires, in certain states anyway. Cable chains do not have the same bite as regular chains. Will is not a big fan of cable chains but says they do have their place if used correctly in certain situations.
We have a nice little system. I put the chains on the tires and Will connects them and cinches them up. You have to lay on the ground to do that part. I usually get a couple of chains connected before Will takes over. Scuba diving gloves work best. They are water proof without being all puffy. One time this female driver comes up to Will, I'm on the other side of the trailer connecting them, and she asks Will if he would help her put chains on, 'it's really cold, her gloves got wet, her fingers are frozen and she has been here for 2 hours' Will said ask my wife she's under the trailer, see if she wants to stay out here any longer. She never asked me. Will said she didn't even have a good warm jacket or boots.

Taking chains off is not as quick as you might think. Most of the time Will wants to carefully rehang the chains, so they are not tangled up for next time. But depending on how much time we lost, how behind we are, once in a while we just hang them up and next day when we have more time he lays them out and hangs them up nice and neat.

Will, telling me to put down the camera and pick up some chains.

The road is always sloppy. When we put chains on, cars never pull off the road enough, sometimes stopping in the middle of the lane to put chains on. Cars also don't slow down when they pass us putting our chains on. The spray is kicking up rocks. It frustrates me that cars are not always required to chain up like trucks are, even though studies show that, in 75% of car vs. semi accidents, the car is at fault.

Drive safe.

Love and miss you all

On the Streets of Laredo

We picked up a load in North Bend, Washington going to Laredo, Texas. We picked it up at Nintendo of America.

There was a lot of security on this load. It was videotaped while being loaded. There were two seals put on the trailer doors, along with our pad lock. The load instructions said we had to drive 200 miles before stopping. If we did not have the hours, or the fuel to drive 200 miles, do not accept this load. One of the team drivers must be with the load at all times. The security guard escorted us to the trailer, watched us hook up, and then made sure we found the exit gate. We had to send a message every time we stopped. Explaining where we were, why we stopped and how long we thought we would be stopped. Then another message when we were rolling again.

When we get to Laredo we had to have the trailer inspected before delivering because it's going into Mexico. We are not taking it to the finale delivery we are dropping at a freight forwarder. As fate would have it we lost one of the trailer brakes. The air canister was slowly leaking but holding air. So Will pulled into a truck stop, called break down and the canister fixed. It's faster to be at a truck stop to get any repair done, than it is to call from a rest area. When they have to send someone it always takes hours.

Another funny twist of fate had me driving in Texas. Not a good plan. I don't know why directions don't work when I read them. I was supposed to turn on Farm Road 179. When I did I kept following it never seeing my next turn anywhere. Then the road was going to turn into a hospital. I had to wake up Will, here we go again. Part of the problem was there is a lot of construction around here and our gps had problems too. Wanting me to turn on roads that were closed, then only wanting me to "Make a U-Turn if possible"

I read the directions.

The directions are in English.

I can understand English.

I can read the road signs,

I see the sign with an arrow that says turn here, and somehow it never works out the way it should. I just don't know why I get so lost. After Will woke up within 15 minutes we were headed the right direction. WTH is wrong with me.

We are staying 3 miles from the Mexico border. We are off for a little shopping. I got 2 water bottle size bottles of vanilla for $2. Some tile crosses, some bracelets for the grand-daughters and maracas for all the kids. What a deal. We could see the Mexican flag as we walked down the street. I'm going to see if we can find an ABC station because as you know, today is not just Thursday, it's Lostday

Love and miss you all.

Don't Do Dover

We are off to Dover Delaware. The First
State. Good, the weather will be cooler. That's
where we will spend our 34 off. Guess what, its
82', Dover is having a heat wave. They love it,
just my luck. The hotel in Dover is a Comfort
Inn. That being said, I beg, I warn everyone not
to stay here. They were nice and let us check in
at 7am, normally check in is 2 or 3 pm. Our
refrigerator in the truck died so we have to
throw out all the food that is in there, replace the
refrigerator and the food. We stop at a big Wal-
Mart, but it's not open yet, 3 weeks until the
grand opening. We find another Wal-Mart's and
it has a small refrigerator. But no groceries.
Have to stop at Safeway.

The room is very musty smelling and
the window is painted shut so we leave the door
open. I grab the laundry bag from the truck and
head straight to the laundry room. The desk
clerk told us when we checked in to come see
her and she would give me a laundry room key.
So I did and she points the way, it is in a
separate building not attached to the hotel but in
the parking lot. The door is open when I get
there and there is only one washer and one
dryer. UGH, I have two loads. I shut the door
and go back to the room. About half an hour
later I went to change the laundry and the key
won't work. I went in a told the desk clerk and
she looked at me funny and said, "Well who
shut the door?"

I told her, I did. Isn't that why you gave me a key, so I could open it when I come back? She got someone in housekeeping to come over with me and see if she could get it open. No luck. Then someone else tried, again no luck. They both left and I waited thinking they were going to solve this problem. But about 10 minutes later I see the housekeeper come out of one of the rooms. I go back to the desk clerk and she said "It's still not open?" She said she could call someone and get them to open it from the inside. So I go back and wait. And wait. AND WAIT. About 20 minutes later I go back to the desk clerk I just open the door and stare at her and she said the lady is on her way, she was on the road and will be right back.

I said, not so politely, I hope so; I have more to do today than just hang out and wait for the laundry room to be opened. Why on earth do you let the only laundry room key leave the hotel? About 15 minutes later the door opens from the inside. The lady didn't say, here you go, sorry about that, nothing. I changed the laundry and grabbed a big overstuffed chair from the driveway (I think it was for sitting on when smoking) and I block the door open.

I get back to the room, my face is all red from sweating and swearing and I see a sock on the floor. I was mad that the sock fell out of the laundry bag, then I remembered I didn't bring the laundry into the room. I went straight to the laundry room from the truck. That sock must have been left here. Oh great and I guess the toe nail clipping under the sock belongs to the owner. I was so mad. I brought the sock and the toe nail down to the front desk and left it there.

No one was there for me to talk to. I whipped out a complaint letter to the hotel and to the chain headquarters.

After Delaware it was off to Arizona.

Where our good luck continued. I had a blowout. I was thankful that the next rest stop was actually open. Most of Arizona's rest stops are closed. Only had a 3 ½ hour wait in the Arizona sun. This sign is in most rest stops in Arizona, New Mexico and Texas.

We did see a semi rear end a car. Not sure exactly what happened. Either the delivery truck was following

too close or the car was already stopped on the side of the road.
Either way, drive careful out there guys.

I love and miss you all.

And Then She Hit Me

I was driving through Oklahoma City and we had about 3 hours before it was time to change drivers.

I saw up ahead a car had merged onto the freeway and merged a little too far crossing into the next lane, causing a few cars to swerve out of her way. So of course most of the trucks slowed down and fell in line behind her. She seemed to drive straight for a while so, slowly trucks started to pass her. I started to pass her and she started to swerve into my lane. I slowed down, hoping she would get in front of me, and got as far over to the left as I could. But not far enough. And then she hit me, she ran into my trailer.

Will was sitting in the passenger seat yelling**, SHES GOING TO HIT YOU, SHES COMING INTO YOUR LANE!!!**

That was scary to watch. I was trying to drive as far left as possible, and not hit the guard rail, but still see what she was doing. I thought for sure she was going to go under the trailer. I could see the cars behind me swerving to avoid what they expected to be an awful crash.

We pulled over to the side of the road. The whole time Will is saying, "There goes <u>our</u> job", "There goes <u>your</u> license"...Very helpful all his positive feedback

you can see her mirror is busted off. The black marks are from my trailer tires hitting the side of her car.

Another car pulled over behind the lady that hit us. He said he's been behind her since she got on the freeway and called 911, warning them she was a hazard, and

was on the phone with them now.

It wasn't long before the Sherriff showed up. Then another. I had to notify our dispatch about the accident. The sheriff took our information, pictures, and then said it was 100% her fault. I did not get a citation at all.

The guy that stopped said he used to be a truck driver. (They're everywhere) You can see from the pictures, the damage to her car is from the tires of the trailer. You can see how scary it must have been for her, as well as me. How easily she could have gone under the trailer and been killed. I could have lost control and hit another car, while trying to avoid her. I could have driven too far over to the left and hit the guard rail and lost control. Lots of things could have gone wrong, glad it went right.

Please drive safe everyone. That lady was not drunk. She was not on her cell phone. She was just a confused grandma.

Love and Miss you all.

Home time Sweet Home time

Home time was great. It feels like I was busy, but didn't get everything accomplished.

We made it home for us to have Will's Birthday dinner (53) with the kids and their respective others. We went to Los Dos Amigo's. Nice time.

Saturday was a long planned and much needed Adams Family Girls day out with Mom, and my sisters Sally and Theresa. Being St. Patrick's Day was the icing on the cake. We left early so we could go to Kells Irish Pub. They throw money on the ceiling all year long and then scrap it down and donate to a local Children s Charity. It's magic how they get it to stick to the ceiling. This year they donate close to $18,000. But the line was too long so we had to scratch that off our list. Don't worry we did get green beer and bagpipes at the Thirsty Lion Pub and Grill.

Then it was off to the main event. Wicked. If you haven't seen it...SEE IT!!!! It was Sally's 3rd time, my 2nd and mom and Theresa's first time. But hopefully it won't be our last. If you have been living under a rock, Wicked is the behind the scene story to the Wizard of Oz. What made the wicked witch, wicked? Why is she green? How does she know Glenda? "..That's Glenda with a Gla..." What's up with the ruby slippers? Can't tell you, don't want to spoil it.

Sunday was our Corned Beef and Cabbage night. It was good, but think next year we will try Lamb Shepherd's Pie

Our middle daughter came home and told us she and her boyfriend are planning to Elope. We are so happy. He is a great guy. Not sure you are supposed to tell people when you're eloping but I don't know what the rules are anymore. She has been single again over a year now, we

are glad she waited to meet the right man. We went with them, met the in-laws they are great too. We just love him. He is so intelligent, respectful, and protective of Jennifer and her 2 daughters, it's nice to know there are still guys out there like him. Oh and by the way he has 1 daughter so the estrogen level in his house just sky rocketed, anyone wanting to time share man cave hours with him I'm sure he'd appreciate it. We are proud and lucky to have both of our son's in law as part of our family.

We got the truck back from the shop. Had to have brakes put on and get the a/c fixed (AGAIN?!?!)

Cost of brakes $290
Cost of A/C $800
Cost of keeping your cool in Texas, Priceless.

Our first trip after home time was to Phoenix. Nice little test for the air conditioner. It passed, almost. It works up front but still blows hot air in the sleeper, even with the a/c off. Only the driver stays cool. That is really bad for Will, which means he is trying to sleep during the day with no air conditioning and the heater slightly on. When it's already 79' there really is no such thing as the heater slightly blowing hot air. Well can't wait to see what happens next.

Love and miss you all

Beale Street in Memphis

I just couldn't wait to tell you about Memphis. Beale Street in Down Town Memphis is open for business. If you don't know about Beale Street you'll have to Google it, I will not be able to explain it properly. The very fact that some of the most talented and influential people in music, not only the blues, have walked down this street is something to think about. It is amazing to think that I was walking down the same street as BB King, Johnny Lee Hooker, Etta James, Muddy Waters, Taj Mahal, Elvis Presley, Johnny Cash, Jerry Lee Lewis, Stevie Ray Vaughan, even Jimmy Buffett, oh my gosh the list goes on and on

We were going to take a tour of downtown, but it was only a 3 hour tour (..... a 3 hour tour) and then we didn't know what we would do the rest of the day. We took a taxi to mid-town, thinking down town was flooded. Mid town just looked like any other down town. We decided to  walk the 6 or 8 blocks to the trolley that would take us close to Beale Street.

We stopped at a place that was advertised as Memphis best pizza. I hope that is not the best Memphis has to offer.

We kept walking and went into the Dubliners Pub. Will had a Guinness and I had pale ale. Then we walked on, finally getting to the trolley stand. It's only a dollar to ride, so everyone should do it.

The trolley was not able to go as far as it normally does; it had to stop because of some historic flooding by the Mississippi river. So we got off and followed the direction of the rest of the riders, they must know where they're going right? Eventually we end up at the Mississippi River. Staring at the flooding with everyone else.

This is usually a street you can walk down

We took some pictures of the flooding. We could see the tops of road signs etc. Half way through our walkabout Will turns to me and says, "Wow the sun really doesn't like you, does it". I said where have you been the last 29 years? My face was all flushed, my arms were red. Will thought another beer was what I needed; I said no some shade and water please.

There were a lot of neat businesses around here. A lot of upscale restaurants and sports bars. We went into one place called The Bluefin. Fancy smancy, not sure we should have been allowed in there. Then we continued walking and next thing you know we are on the famous Beale Street.

Wow

My heart skipped a beat. I love blues music. The first building that caught my eye was BB King's night club.

I am not worthy…I am not worthy

BB King   Elvis Presley
The Blues Brothers

The line was around the corner so we thought we would try on our way back. There is no car traffic in this part of town.

There are over 100 brass music notes embedded on the sidewalks of Beale Street. They honor past and present individuals for their contribution to both blues music and their part in putting Beale Street on the world music map.

The police have the connecting roads barricaded and you can walk and drink and dance your way from one end of Beale Street to the other. If you get tired of walking you can

take a horse and carriage ride. One restaurant was advertising, BBQ chicken, baked beans and deep fried apple pie....all I could think was HONEY, I'M HOME!!!

There was music playing everywhere live bands playing on corners, in the bars, and in the parks. We went into one park and sat down while a band was setting up. We got there just in time. Once they started playing the place filled up. The band was the Plantation All Stars. Very good. Nothing better than live blues music. We thought there were a lot of roadies for the band until we saw the manager keep shoeing people off the stage. One guy even gave the singer a beer, hung around on stage before he was taken off.

When they stopped for a break we went looking for a bathroom. We went into a place where they were selling Cuban cigars? But I thought that was illegal. That was not the only illegal stuff going on. Just sitting in the park we are questionable about passing any surprise drug test. Patchouli oil does not cover the smell of everything people take a bath and get high in your own house. Anyway looking at the sign closer it said Cuban <u>seed</u> cigars. What are they?

We decided to eat dinner on the way out. BB King's still had a long line so we stopped at Pig on Beale, Pork with Attitude. I had the chicken, Will had pork ribs. Not a lot of overhead here, paper plates and plastic wear, but good food.

I had a wonderful time in Memphis, even though we were in between festival weekends. Last weekend was the music festival and next weekend is the BBQ festival. Will was wondering what we will do next time our 34 off falls in Memphis, I'm thinking BEALE STREET. Maybe on a weekday we can get into BB King's.

I can't wait to come back.

Love and miss you all

Sleepless in the Semi

The wind was unreal again in Wyoming. Will woke me to sit up front. He thinks it's safer even though I use the safety net in the sleeper. He says, look at every truck accident, roll over or jackknife and the trailer usually comes around and crushes the sleeper berth. The wind was so bad and blowing so much dirt you couldn't see the road. Will finally made it to a rest area and we parked there for a few hours until the wind died down a bit. I still thought it was too windy but Will said it was better now. Good enough to drive in but not good enough to go back to the sleeper.

Both of us, sleeping in the sleeper is quite a dance. If it's just for a few hours like this time then we can sleep like normal people. Well, two normal people sleeping in a twin size bed. If it's sleeping for 10 hours or so, we sleep head to toe. It's hard to get comfortable either way. It's hard for me to sit up and read when Will is trying to sleep.

Almost as hard as it is to sleep in the front seat.

Love and miss you all

Tornado and Flooding

We have been getting some good miles the last 2 weeks, (I know, I hate to jinx it) our reloads have been coming fairly quick so not a lot of sitting time. Maybe my letter did some good. Not a lot of time to blog either. We got a load from Yuma, Arizona to Blythewood, South Carolina. Then picked up one going to Santa Fe Springs, California.

Driving through Texas, Will is always pointing out property. 20 acres for $16,500. He really thinks this is where we should spend our twilight years. I promised to write him.

Both loads took us through some of the recent tornado damage area. Not through Tuscaloosa, Alabama, but through Birmingham and Adamsville. I remember taking pictures last year in Adamsville because I thought it might be a nice place for all us Adams's to live, Will included.

The tornado pictures do not do the damage justice.

And we only went past a small one. It was very sobering to drive by and see down trees on the right side of the street, and then on the left side no house left un- touched.

The tornado went right across the highway. I didn't get a good parking spot at the viewing site, so I didn't get pictures from the best view, but I think you will agree the damage is devastating. A block away is the water treatment plant, un touched. And further up the road is a lumber yard, untouched. Can you imagine 2x4's and 4x4's flying around. Oh my gosh.

Also got a few pictures of flooding in West Memphis, Arkansas, just on the other side of the Mississippi River from Memphis, Tennessee.

The flood waters are moving so slow. Living in Oregon, when it floods, it floods fast and usually subsides quickly within a few days or a week. Most of our soil is like a sponge and soaks up water. But this is still flooding. It will continue to rise for a few more weeks and then stay for a while.

They are saying a couple of months. Making planting season for farmers touch and go.

They are saying it took weeks for the flood the hit its high mark and it will take weeks after that to go down. One news reporter said the Mississippi flood waters in Louisiana should subside just in time for hurricane season. That's crazy.

We are driving on I40 west bound. It had been closed for about 2 weeks because of the flooding. Glad it's open now. It was a 150 mile detour.

So all in all, Oregon is not such a bad place. No earthquakes, no hurricanes, no slow moving floods, no killer snow storms. Just rain. In case you want to attend the Oregon Rain Festival it is held, Jan 1 – Dec 31.

Well that's not fair, we do get about 60 days of no rain. But its normal rain, not this crazy rain out here. And people know how to drive in the rain. They don't stop in the middle of the road. They don't put the hazards lights on and drive 10 mph. They don't all pile up and stop under the over pass waiting for it to stop, because it isn't going to.

 Love and miss you all.

I Hate Driving

I hate being gone all the time. Not being there for little events in my grandkids life; graduation from kindergarten, testing for black belt, dance recitals, or to babysit. I hate not being around to help my kids or even just sit and talk and laugh with them. I hate not being home and able to run over and see my mom and dad on the spur of the moment. I miss the dog. I miss not being able to be with family when they are sick. I hate only communicating with family and friends through text or email. I hate being mad at someone and only being able to get 3 feet away. It is impossible to fully convey your anger by slamming a curtain shut.

I hate not eating normal meals. Having to run and look for a rest stop, having to grab an extra pair of pants when I run into the rest stop because I already know I'm not going to make it. I didn't think I would, but I hate not exercising. Running to the bathroom doesn't count. All I do is move from the driver's seat to the sleeper.

What I like about driving. Paying the bills; let me get back to you on the rest of that.

There, now I feel better.

Driving through New Mexico, there is a ton of smoke. Not from a fire here but a huge fire in Arizona. The smoke was so thick we had to turn our head lights on. For a brief moment I thought we were back in Oregon and it was field burning season. Will is sleeping comfortably in the sleeper, covered up with a blanket and sleeping with his socks on. That's how cold it is in the sleeper.

But it is hot as hell up in the drivers' area. He is hogging all the coolness by keeping the Curtin closed. If you detect a hint of sarcasm, you are correct my dear. The air conditioning in the cab is not working, AGAIN. I have been complaining about it for a couple of months. I know it was not summer a couple of months ago, but needed to use it a couple of times. Will said I must have been having a hot flash. A HOT FLASH. Yes that's what he said.

He has recently seen the light and has come to his senses. Now he agrees with me that it isn't working as good as it should.

Duh!! Hot flash, I'm much too young for that.

Love and miss you all

R.I.P Sgt. Schultz Zeppelin

When we left we had a feeling Schultz would only have about a year or so left. We wondered if he would make it through another winter. His arthritis is bad. It is as painful for him to get up and down as it is for us to watch him. He has a large tumor on his chest. Last year we asked the doctor about it. We thought it was extra muscle because he is forced to use his front legs more because of his back leg. The vet thought that at first too. But then a few months later when we brought him in, it had grown and she was able to determine it was not muscle. Because of his age, 13 we decided to watch it, and watch him.

Willy and Schultz at Saint Francis for the blessing of the animals

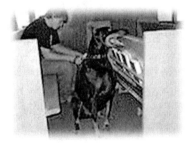

Willy called and said it sounded like Schultz was breathing through a straw under water. I called Paige, (she used to work for the Vet) and she set up an in home visit. Willy did not think Schultz would be able to get in and out of the car. Dr. Dore came to the house and agreed that it was time. My wonderfully caring son-in-law Jeff helped Willy. It was so hard not being there to help our son or let Schultz know one last time how much we love him.

Schultz kepping Lilly Compnay in time out

Shultz was a great dog. He sometimes forgot he was a Doberman and thought he was a herding dog. Every time the grandkids would be outside running around, Schultz would look like he's playing with them, chasing them etc. But in no time at all the kids would be yelling,

"Grandma!!!", "Schultz won't let us play" We would look out to see the kids in the corner and Schultz would sit in front of them looking at us, proud of his accomplishment. Just like an Australian Shepard and a bunch of sheep. All the while Schultz was thinking they are easier to protect when in one place.

Sometimes he would think he was a black and tan hound dog. He killed Opossums that wondered into our yard. And one stray bunny rabbit.

He was always fighting a losing battle trying to keep Blue Jays out of HIS apple tree.

He loved those apples. At the end of the season, in the snow, freezing rain or hail, he would be out, eating the last of the apples on the ground. It was hard to harvest the apples because he would pick them out of the basket we just put them in. He was an apple-holic.

One time during a water gun fight out back, grandpa used the hose on the kids. They started screaming. I mean SCREAMING. Schultz came running, full speed, quickly surveying the scene and stood between grandpa and the kids. Every time grandpa took a step towards the girls, Schultz stood his ground. Keeping himself between the girls and grandpa.

He was great with the grandkids. He let them crawl all over him, dress him up, take naps with him. He would always run back and forth between us and the room where a baby was crying, as if we

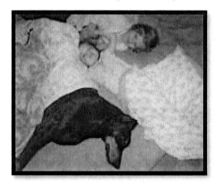

couldn't hear. When one of the kids would have a toddler melt down. If you picked the kid up to move them to another room, Schultz would start whinnying. He would follow you down the hall, nudging his nose in between you and the crying kid. He would jump up and pinch your elbow. (Not bite, pinch).

He would try to pull the child away from us. You could read his mind. You just know he was thinking. 'I know I suppose to protect the little ones, I know I'm not supposed to bite the hand that feeds me…but the little one doesn't act like they are helping him….'

Schultz was laid to rest under the grape arbor, next to 'his' apple tree.

Love and miss you all

Open Letter from My Truck to All Cars

Since I have been saying daily prayers to St Christopher, I don't have any oh crap I got lost stories, but my truck would like to say a few words.

HANG UP THE DAMN PHONE AND NOTICE THE 75 FOOT LONG HOUSE DRIVING BESIDE YOU !

WTH is the problem with you and merging? It really is not that hard. You cars can all stop quicker and accelerate quicker than I can. It is **YOUR** responsibility to MERGE. When getting on the freeway **YOU** are in the **MERGE** lane. Heck sometimes there is a sign that reminds you to merge. That signs faces you **not** me. Your lane is ending, not mine. The word merge means blend, not force. The freeway traffic always has the right of way. The freeway traffic is under no obligation to slow down or change lanes to accommodate merging traffic.

I cannot quickly change lanes and jerk the truck over to the left lane to let you in. I risk becoming unstable perhaps even rolling on top of you, because of you. If there is room I will change lanes. And I thank you when you change lanes and allow me to merge safely. When I do move over to let you in, please let me back in the right hand lane. In most states I can get a ticket for driving out in the left lane for too long. My driver cannot afford a ticket for being nice. If I am able let you in, please reciprocate and let me back in the right lane. I cannot stop to let you on the freeway, just because you could not decide whether to go in front or behind me. Make a decision and stick with it.

Did you know it takes about 400 feet for me to stop when traveling 55mph.

And when was the last time you saw a truck do 55. It takes 40% longer for me to stop than it does for you to stop.

DO NOT continue to drive beside me until your lane ends, then flip me off. It's not my driver's problem your driver can't merge. Another issue related to merging. When, because of road work, accident, police activity or any other reason the number of lanes reduces, do not wait till the last possible second to merge. You just hold up traffic. You are not any more important than the person you are trying to get in front of. Come on, you know this one, you learned it in kindergarten, get in line, and take turns. No cutting

We leave a space between us and the vehicle in front of us to allow for stopping time, not for you to cut in front of us. That's our safety cushion. We need that space. If you refuse to merge early and help traffic continue to roll smoothly, a couple of trucks will help remind you there is a merge ahead. We will drive side by side each other until you merge into the correct lane. Then we can all continue on our merry way.

As long as I have your attention; when my driver turns on the blinker; that is not a signal for you to speed up. That's how I know you saw my blinker, you speed up. It means for whatever reason I need that lane. Maybe because there is a police car on the right shoulder, a stopped car, a hitchhiker or a three toed sloth, the point is, at that moment it is **illegal** and more important **unsafe** for me to drive in the right hand lane. I'm not getting in the left lane just to get in front of you; I am not trying to ruin your view. (**It's not always about you**) I'm not trying to get there before you, and as soon as I pass the problem I will move back to the right hand lane, that is if you are not trying to zip around me and pass me on the right. So my left blinker isn't always a request for your permission to move to the left lane, it's more of an announcement, **I need to move over,** and since I saw you speedup, I know you saw my blinker so **here I come.**

Ladies and I use that term loosely. Don't drive up, lift your shirt and show us your boobs.

Only one of my drivers is slightly amused anyway.

If you don't need a bra my driver does not consider them boobs.

My driver loves and misses you all

How Many Guys Does It Take To Unlock a Truck?

The answer is about 5. We stopped to get the truck washed and when I got out I locked the door. When Will got out, he did not take the keys. When the truck was done, we could not get in. Of course every guy in the joint was looking and shaking their heads  at me. Patting Will on the shoulder, sympathizing with his life... Poor Will. I asked Will if he wanted some crackers with that whine. Turns out all truck keys are not universal anymore, a slim jim is not quit slim enough, and a coat hanger is not strong enough to raise the lock. Eventually another new International truck came in and the key opened the door. Everybody waved and cheered when we finally left.

Love and miss you all

Occupy Oakland, Dead Starter, What's Next?

We made it out of Oakland safe and sound. We were down by the docks but did not have to pick up there this time. We were on the freeway that was shown on the news. Good thing we were in and out in the morning.

I tell you watching it on TV; I was scared for those truck drivers. The whole time I kept thinking of Reginald Denny, the truck driver that was pulled out of his truck during a riot in LA. And nearly beaten to death. It was so long ago, in the 90's I think, I don't think it was in the 80's. The whole thing was caught on tape by a news-chopper. I'm so glad nothing like that happened in Oakland.

There have been a couple of times, Will has told me to get in the back. (Sleeper), delivering to a very bad neighborhood. Guys walking up and down the middle of the street, looking in cars as if to find an easy one to car jack, tagging trailers right there at the stop lights. One business we had to rush to get to before they closed because they lock the gate and the guard doesn't let anyone in. And that was one area you do not want to be left out on the street. I remember the lot inside was full of trucks. Most were there 12 hours early just so they could be locked inside safe for the night.

The truck is in the shop. Again. This time it's for the starter, shocks, airbags, and air conditioner and to figure out why the check engine light is on. Yes I made sure the gas cap was on tight, silly. The starter went out fast, without any warning. We had a hard time starting it once in Salt Lake City. Will told me not to turn the truck off, and we'd get it checked later. After we left Oakland, we stopped in Livermore and I shut the truck off. It would not start.

Will looked at it but where it is he couldn't get to it. We called White Trucking and asked if they can come and give us a pull start.

Of course you knew they can't push start a tractor-trailer. White Trucking said they don't have the equipment. We thought we had 1 free tow available from International, so we called them and they had no idea what we were talking about. $$ OUCH. $$ We were on the phone ordering a tow and it started. I didn't mind cashing in karma points for that.

We went to the White Trucking shop in Lathrop and told them the issues and they said they could fix it; most of it would be warranty work, cool beans.

So here we sit at the hotel. Will sleeping, me with nothing to do. No book. I finished, Cleopatra's Daughter, very good. And I am out of yarn so I can't work on the sweater. The last 3 Wal-Mart's did not have the yarn. I have more at the house; but that doesn't do me any good here does it.

We got the truck back from White Trucking/Lathrop. They said all was fixed. We looked at the paper work and they did not fix the starter because it started. They did fix something with the check engine light, even though that light came on 20 miles down the road. Still no fix for the broken A/C

Next stop International in Springfield Oregon. We put the truck in there, same problems, same results. They can't get the starter to fail so they can't fix it under warranty. They did spend a lot time and fixed they real problem with the check engine light. Of course not a warrantee fix, out of pocket. We told them to replace the starter and we'll pay out of pocket for that too. It's only money. We can't have it only fail on us. As soon as they heard we were going to fork over $1000 they oet right on it.

Our son is down in San Diego for some for 'Magic the Gathering' card show/tournament, he loves it. Says it is definitely on his list of places to live. We were just glad to hear that we are not the only place on his list.

Love and miss you all,

Gone with the Wind, Almost

Oh My Gosh it was so windy. We are taking a Cabela's load from Springfield Oregon to Salt Lake City and then to their headquarters in Sidney, Nebraska. It's a neat run, good enough miles and it's a round trip dedication. White Trucking is trying to get us to sign on to this dedicate route. Will doesn't want to be stuck on this route during the winter. Anyway, it was so windy in Wyoming; I know you're thinking when it is not windy. The driver behind me came on the CB 'White Trucking, your bouncing like ball, they don't have you dead-heading in this weather do they?' Deadhead is when you are hauling an empty trailer on the way to pick up a load. I said 'might as well be, I only have 18 in the box.' (18,000 lbs.'). He came back and said 'Well miss White (I like how they call me Miss White when being helpful, much better than the other names I've been called) why don't you scoot over and I'll come up beside you and we can both get down this hill' So I got in the left lane and he came up and drove beside me on the right, blocking the wind.

When you're empty or light your trailer is just like a big sail. After a few miles he said to drive safe, I told him thanks for the help and just like that my friendly wind block left. That was nice.

Will said truckers used to do a lot more of that. Stopping to help someone with a flat tire, etc. Truckers used to be called Knights of the road. Now because of new laws making stopping on side of road ticketable, shorter time lines from companies and the overall feeling you might be being set up by load-hijacker, truckers don't stop like they used to. The times they are a changin'.

Love and miss you all

Just Another Man Impressed With My Driving

You have all been so patient, faithfully reading my blogs. Hoping one day I would demoralize and humiliate myself with another lost story. Well your patience has paid off.

This trip had everything I dread. Airports and New Jersey. Throw in Texas and you'd win the daily trifecta.

Our first load was going to UPS at the Philadelphia airport. There is construction and

detours everywhere, which only add to my confusion. But the drive into Philadelphia was fine. I was following the directions from White Trucking and it wasn't long before I was staring at the arrival/departure parking garage. Same problem, different airport.

I stopped to ask the guard, with the horrified look on  his face, how to get to Hog Island Road? He pointed behind us and to the left. When I asked if we could go straight ahead, he said "I don't see how." Not nearly as helpful as when I get going the wrong way at the Salt Lake City airport. They had a guard come up to me and help me get turned around. Salt Lake airport is the place to get lost if you have a semi.

I forgot to mention, I was stopped in 1 lane of 4, all going one way, and we need to go the other way......Where is the rapture when I need it?

So Will gets out to spot for me while I back up about 1000 feet and just like that we are headed in the right direction. We thought. The new directions take us right back to the passenger terminals. Been there, done that. But Will sees a road that looks like it goes around the back of the airport. It does and soon we find a UPS truck and follow him. What can brown do for you? It can lead the way, that's what. And soon we are at UPS.

UPS doesn't have an empty trailer to swap out for our loaded one. White Trucking sends us to New Jersey to look for one. Like there is not an empty trailer anywhere closer.

I'll make this part short. We were supposed to go to Ocean Spray for an empty trailer. The directions sounded easy, only a couple of turns. Turns out the address White Trucking gave me, is for deliveries, the empties are a few blocks away. Only one wrong turn, and since I was bob-tailing I didn't have to drag a trailer around town with me. One hint that I'm driving where I shouldn't be is people stop and look at me like I'm from Mars. And everyone was staring at me now. I had turned into a park because the bridge in front of me was only 10ft high. I need at least 13'6" and even then I duck when I drive under. That's right, Stop playing ball, stop pushing your kids on the swings, and just stare at the lost truck driver. At any rate I need to be at the other end of Park Street ....HEY WHITE TRUCKING........North, East, South or West would be a nice touch on the address.

**note to self, buy more lottery tickets
I finally get an empty, now I am off to The Christmas Tree Shop.

This is where it gets interesting.
Ok, everybody unfold your New Jersey map or
Log into Google Street View, or Map-Quest.
 Go ahead I'll wait...
Everybody ready? Good. Now look for this
address
270 Daniels Street, Florence NJ.
What? You can't find it in Florence? Keep
looking.
 Never mind
Try Daniels Way in Burlington City.
Now here are the directions White Trucking sent
me.
Go south on US130 (5miles)
Right on Delaware Ave (CR656) (1.5 mile)
Left on Broad Street
Left on East 3rd Street
 * **Arrive at destination, Christmas Tree Shops,
270 Daniels Street Florence, NJ
        NO!!!!!
        I have arrived at a small residential
neighborhood. Oh my, the people were staring
at me now. Beautiful neighborhood seems nice
and quiet, till the semi (with a trailer now)
showed up. Oh hey look how low those power
lines hang, that can't be legal, or safe for me.
One guy on a bicycle turned around and
followed me. This was pretty easy since I was
going so slow trying to decide how to get the
hell out of there. He was waving his hand so I
stopped. He asked what I was looking for. I told
him. He said "a big warehouse, right?" I nodded
my head (I didn't really know I just guessed it
wasn't here at Mr. & Mrs. Nussbaum's
driveway) then he asked how I got in here.

~ 136 ~

Just another man impressed with my unique driving skills.

He said he doesn't even drive his motor home down this street!

Well now he's just flattering me. I think he is flirting.

Turns out he's a firefighter and knew where I wanted to go. His directions were right on the money. Thank You, New Jersey's finest!! We arrive safely and pick up our loaded trailer and head for Augusta, Georgia. Leaving town was pretty easy. Almost.

You know how most people have an internal compass? Well my internal compass is stuck on shipyard. Must be the sailor's daughter in me.

**A lot more lottery tickets

Well that was just a little site seeing trip, hardly even out of the way. The important thing to remember is nobody got hurt. To top off a perfect day I listened to the Civil War.

Beavers vs. Ducks.

In reality, Beaver Nation knew the season would end this way. The same way it started. We may be the giant killers, so there was always a little hope. But I am still a Beaver Believer. I bleed orange, (except on St Paddy's day)

Finale score Beavers 21 Ducks 49. Just wait till next year. Then we'll shut the duck up!!!

After Augusta, we pick up a load going to Memphis. Memphis, we were just there for Thanksgiving. We ate at a Piccadilly Cafeteria. We ended up having to wait 24 hours before picking up the load that started this whole adventure.

While in Memphis we went to a gas station across the street from our hotel and Will bought beer. He was carded! My 53 year old gray bearded husband was carded. I don't think Barbie could even count to 21. We walk back to the hotel and stop to get stuff out of the truck. While Will is walking across the parking lot some little Suzie Q stops her car and asks Will if he needed a date? He said he had one and pointed to the room?

WHAT? Oh NO he didn't. What did he say? Did he mean me? After 29 years, I'm just the date waiting in the hotel room? I should be charging him more. Maybe this is my way out; after all it's just a date.

So I had to put up with his inflated ego the rest of the day, and the next day.....Now really I don't mind some young thing stroking his ego, since I usually receive the benefit of that, as long as that's all they stroke!

I love and miss you all

This Job Sucks

I hate truck driving. I hate the way the dispatchers treat you. I hate the way the company you work for treats you. I hate the way the other drivers treat you. I hate the way the law treats the drivers. Truck drivers are only *allowed* to work 70 hours a week. 70 hours without overtime. We don't get paid for all those hours either.

You've heard it before, If the wheels aint turnin' I aint earnin'. A truck driver can drive 11 hours a day, but I can work 14 hours day. The law does say I have to have 10 hours off before I can drive again. That's very nice of them. Everything you do working is free. You only get paid to drive. A flatbed driver, strapping and tarping his load, that work is done for free. Unless he gets tarping pay. He's only getting paid to drive. So doing a pretrip on your truck is counted as working, not driving time. Fueling, going to the bathroom, washing the windows, breaking ice off your wipers, putting chains on, taking chains off, that all counts as working not driving. Sitting in traffic, sometimes waiting at shipper depends on what you are doing, stopped because of an accident, driving slow because of weather, getting lost due to dispatcher's directions, arriving at the wrong time because of dispatcher's information counts as driving time.   We get paid by the mile. Next time you are stuck in stopped traffic because of an accident, think of the truck you are parked next to. You might be late getting home from work, but that driver is now making $ zero.

When traffic gets rolling at a snail's pace then that driver is raking in about .45 cents an hour.

Tell me another job where you are 'allowed' to work 70 hours a week and not get paid overtime. The rest of jobs have a 40 hour work week. You don't get paid if a load cancels. You wasted all that time driving. That time is off your logs. Now you have no place to go. Or we arrive to pick up a load and the weight is incorrect and you can't haul it. The law and most companies have time limits on how long you're allowed to idle.

And don't even get me started on the bathroom situations. I hate when shippers won't let you use their bathroom, it's for employees only. I hate having Will stand guard at the men's bathroom because the woman's is being cleaned, or there is a line. I hate using the men's bathroom when Will is sleeping because I can't wait to wake him up. I hate having to use 'other than normal' restrooms simply because I can't make it to the bathroom. I hate having to pull over, wake Will up, kick him out of the sleeper and use our garbage/toilet pail.

I hate being away from my family. I hate knowing they need me. I hate needing them and not being able to call. I hate crying and not having anyone to talk to. Why can't I get a normal job?

I HATE IT....I WANT TO QUIT

I miss my family so much, I don't know how other drivers do this.

Hello Lewiston

Our reloads continue to be slow and short miles. They continued to let us sit for 10-12 hours because they needed a Haz-Mat team for a FedEx load. Most of the time the miles are under 1000 not even 2 full shifts for each of us.

We told our DM months in advance that we needed to be home on a certain date. We reminded her weeks in advance. For a week we reminded her daily. We were in El Paso and we would need to leave by the next day in order to make it back home on time. They kept sending us loads that would not work. Some even headed east. I told our DM we stayed out for 4 months to make this home time work. We were not going to miss our daughter's graduation from nursing school because of her incompetence.

I know you can't get home on a certain day; loads just don't work like that. We always put in for a home time date about a week before we really need it. We make any doctor appointments etc. during that following week when White will actually get us home. We did that this time too. But today was our drop dead date. We need to head west now. So we did.

Messages kept coming, telling us we could not move on our own. They kept sending us loads that would not work. They sent us excuses; that we were being unreasonable. They can't make loads just appear. We told them when we get to phoenix we will unload the truck and fly home. We are done.

When we get to Albuquerque they sent us a load. A preloaded trailer sitting in the El Paso, yard going to Seattle. That would have worked. Seattle is about 250 north of Lebanon but we can bobtail home from there. But we were too far away now to accept that load. To add insult to injury, that load was sitting in the El Paso yard while we were there complaining about not having a load. UGH!

When we got to Phoenix they gave us a load to Portland. So we made it home in time for Jennifer's graduation. What a great accomplishment for her. She worked very hard and we are so proud of her.

After several frustrated emails and calls between our DM, our terminal manager, they brought in Mr. COO to help. And he was extremely helpful. He took our concerns to heart and came up with a solution. He wanted us to change terminals. Now we will be dispatched out of the Lewiston, Idaho terminal. Our new DM is also a load planner, so she can do both jobs. Before our DM would send a message to load planners for us. This way we don't have a middle man.

We are excited about the change and our first load is to Ohio. Normally our first load after home time is to Sacramento. So we are off to a good start.

Love and miss you all.

This is What Happens When You Hit a Tire on the Freeway

Looks like we all survived the holidays. (We live to shop another day) We had a great time at home. Spending time with the grandkids is always my favorite time. Watching Christmas from their eyes is wonderful. More Grandkids!!! That's what the world needs.

We headed out from Lebanon to Sacramento, not good miles but at least it got us rolling and into California. From Sacramento we headed to Salt Lake City. From there we got a load to Miami. Finally, some good miles.

The trip was uneventful until I got to Atlanta. It was dark and I hit something on I75. At first I thought the truck passing me had a blow out, but it didn't feel like I ran over rubber, Felt like I hit the Jersey barrier. (Not that I ever hit one..)

I pulled over immediately. Shaking so badly I couldn't turn the radio down. Will looks out of the sleeper

"What the hell was that?"

I told him, I hit something.

You hit something? What?

I don't know. I was really crying by then and shaking more so Will got out. I got out and realized the driver steps are bent up and uneven. Will and I walk back down the freeway looking with the flashlight to see what I hit. We found nothing.

We did find across the freeway on the opposite side 3 vehicles stopped. I told Will that's about where I hit something, but on my side of the freeway. Thank God we did not find another car or motorcycle in the ditch. We walk back to the truck the whole time I'm thinking I really have to pee now. I hope the police hurry and get here so I can give my urine sample. I called to report the accident while Will was checking out the damage, making sure the fuel tank was not compromised, checking the fuel tank straps. Looking under to see what damage was done and doing temporary duct tape repairs.

They told me I didn't have to file a police report because no other vehicle was

involved, no other property was damaged and nobody was injured. (Guess nerves don't count)

Will said there was rubber on the front of truck, on the busted pieces of the flaring, on the fuel tank and a little rubber mark up on my driver's side window. The windshield is cracked, but doesn't look like anything hit it; Will thinks it must be a stress crack.

So he agreed I hit a tire. I said it felt like cement. He said it was probably a truck's spare tire. Some drivers keep their spare mounted on the rim so they can change the tire themselves and not have to pay the call out charge. The noise I heard was probably the tire falling off the truck, not a blowout.

When I calmed down enough and we got all situated and ready to leave we notice there is a police car with the vehicles on the other side of the freeway. I drove over there, since I was headed back to the nearest yard, and talked to the officer. I told him I hit a tire and I have signification damage. I wondered if these cars are related to my problem. He said no they didn't lose a spare, they hit a tire. He checked to make sure I still had mine. Anyway, talking it through we guess what happened. I hit the tire and it flew over to the other side where they hit it. Nobody else on my side stopped. Nobody in front or behind me swerved to avoid debris. Nobody else knew anything happened. Nobody on the CB said watch for out for debris or gator on the road. They're usually pretty good at letting you know that stuff.

Seems weird to me that I would be the only one to hit the tire and it would take off flying horizontal never hitting anything on my side of the freeway and land on the other side damaging other vehicles. But that's the general consensus. Despite what happened I am really blessed. I am so blessed. I didn't hurt anyone and we weren't hurt. So many things could have gone wrong. I hate to think how things would have turned out if the tire would have bounced and came through the windshield.

White says we should return to the Decatur, Georgia yard and have the truck repaired there. They would also get someone to take our load to Miami. Darn, we really needed those miles to Miami, but it takes a day to get a load out of the state.

We get to Decatur the shop tells us they would order the parts and we could be on the road Wednesday. Cool beans. Not too bad. In the morning, they tell us they can't fix it and we would need to take it to Memphis, about 375 miles. Ok so off to Memphis we go. They won't give us a load because of our damage so these are miles we are not getting paid for. Add to that, the cost for the repairs we are just bleeding money again. They suggested we take an empty trailer with us so when we are fixed and road ready we won't have to play hide and seek looking for an empty. I said are you paying us to haul your trailer? They said no. Then, no we are not working for free. So we bobtailed.

That's where we are headed now to Memphis. I think Will is secretly hoping to see Barbie and Suzie Q from our last stay in Memphis.
I'll let you know what happens next.

Love and Miss you all so much.

I had to tell Will his Brother died today

Danny had cancer. He was put on hospice about 3 months ago, so it was not all together unexpected. I got a call from each of Danny's sons and Will and Danny's sister telling me the news. I could not decide whether I should let Will get some sleep and tell him later or should I wake him now. I decided to split the difference and tell him around noon. He said he thought that was why his phone wouldn't stop ringing. He didn't want to talk to anyone.

Danny was a good guy. He had a lot of demons, but if you looked past all that there was a great guy hiding underneath. We could always joke. He could take a joke and not take it personally. It was fun sparing with him. He could keep up his end. Every super bowl Sunday I would say to him, "Danny, tell me of the old days, the days before there was a super bowl".

He was very good with cars, could keep just about anything running, along with his mouth. That man had the gift of gab. If you had not known better you would think he was kissing the blarney stone daily.

This is one of the stories about Danny and Will that gets told a lot. Will, being under 21, stopped by to get his sister in law to buy him, and his friends, some beer. After they got back from the store Janet went back into the house. Will, with his friends, in one of their cars, started to leave, and Danny came home.

Well one thing led to another and Danny started chasing the car full of men leaving his house in a hurry. They sped through town. Danny rear-ending their car, and Will telling his friends to stop because Danny didn't know it was him. The chase continued through the back roads of Plymouth, River Pines and Fiddle Town California. Not as far as it sounds they are all a stone's throw from each other. And eventually Danny decided it was a good idea to fire shots at the car he was chasing.

Yes, I believe alcohol contributed to this decision. Will says once Danny started shooting he quit telling his friend to stop and pull over. The car Will was in crashed. Will said he and Danny had a lot of work to do on that car.

One of my favorite jokes to play on him took a little planning, but was worth it. Whenever we would be drinking even if we went out to a bar I would plan ahead and set this up. I would take a maraschino cherry stem and tie it in a knot and put it in my pocket. Then I would order my vodka sunrise and change the one that came with the drink for the one in my pocket. I would put the pre-knotted stem in my mouth, make a big production moving my mouth, and then teasingly present my hidden talent to Danny. He would flip out. Begging me to do it again. I would tell him just one show per customer. Will would look at Danny, raise his eyebrows and just smile. It worked every time I did it. As time went on I had to put the knotted stem in my mouth before I ordered my drink because Danny was watching me closer and closer. Then it was quite a trick to keep the two stems separate in my mouth.

At one time I thought it would be easier to just learn how to tie the stem in a knot, while in my mouth. But every time I saw Danny laugh I decided this was a better plan.

After I started truck driving, whenever I saw Danny he would say "Hey, you mother trucker how's life on the road" and I would always warn him not to say that too fast. I wouldn't want him getting tongue tied. I'd hate to have to slap him in front of his little brother.

I'm going to miss Danny. I can't believe how hard it must be for Will, to be handling this stuff over the road, being away from his family. We were just home and saw Danny a couple of weeks ago, but still it must be un bearable not to be able to just forget about the world for a day or two. He still has to pay attention to the road, be a safe driver. I hate this job and can't wait till we can quit.

RIP Danny

Love and Miss you all

Rear Window or Cabin Fever, You Decide

Under considerable duress, my oldest daughter is forcing me to write about our recent stay in Memphis.

I wish I could tell you the following is a combination of Alfred Hitchcock's Rear Window, The Soprano's or Sons of Anarchy, with maybe a little cabin fever thrown in. But I'll let you decide. Before that I need to set the scene.

While the truck was in the shop we stayed where we usually stayed. The beautiful, but mostly affordable, Motel 6 on East Brooks in Memphis. The surrounding area sucks. It is mostly industrial. The convenience store across the street has bars on the inside. Everything is behind the glass and bars. You have to tell the clerk, behind the bullet proof glass, what you want, you point to the bread, the chips, the salsa, the beer and after you pay for it they slide it into a lazy Suzanne like thing, spin it and you get your groceries. Only one place delivers to the hotel, Yep, Chinese Food. Not bad food but can't live on it for a week.

There are not even continuous sidewalks. We went for a walk and Will promised it would be to a well-populated, ok area. After about half an hour I tell him I didn't bring my wallet, he said why he has money if I want to buy something. I said no I just don't want the police report to say. And victim B was found over there.

Real newspaper article"....A Memphis strip club was shut for the second time in less than 10 months. Nearby businesses describe "Babes of Babylon" as a haven for drugs, prostitution, and crime. They bring a lot of trouble and we recently got robbed, said the Motel 6 manager Diptesh Patel. In December 2010 the strip joint was shut down for prostitution and drugs...."

Being about 3 miles from Graceland, and about 10 miles from Beale Street, you'd think the area would be a little more upscale or at least clean. So anyway before we check in we go to Wal-Mart, get food to last a week, then we settle in at the hotel. We want to get everything we will need before we put it in the shop. The Hotel is fine. A clean bed, nice shower, refrigerator, microwave and TV.

We always joke about the hotel being next door to the Babylon strip club. Will is always volunteering to go see if they have hot wings there. He's helpful like that.

Well a few hours after we arrived there was a knock on the door. When I answered it the "woman" on the other side looked surprised to see me answer, and asked if I have been in this room a while? I said yes and she said ok and left. HUM? That is Clue # 1

The next night there is a fight in the room next to ours. Not a clue to the mystery just thought you should know we could not hear everything that was said. Very frustrating.

The 3rd night there was a ton of traffic, at the far corner of the hotel. Cars coming and going all night.

I even timed it. Every 20 minutes a black suv would leave and a different car would come and stay for 20 minutes, clue #2. A white delivery van was coming and going in between the 20 minute intervals, clue #3

The 4th day we see the lady a couple rooms down from us out in the parking lot with her mother dog and its litter of puppies, pit bull mix. Trying to sell the puppy's to people who drove in. Not a clue but made a mental note, not to accept room #115.

Will spy's a minivan, parked a couple of doors down from us loaded with hula hoops. And not the normal ones, he says sparkle ones, clue #4. A pink feather is found in the parking lot, clue #5.

A lot of truck drivers have shown up in the last few hours, and you know what they say about truck drivers, clue # 6

**the following is text messages between my daughters and my sister Theresa.

ME: to Paige, Jennifer and Theresa; Dad walks down to the vending machines and hears two guys talking ....'And they got 3 guns over there.' he comes back and double locks the door; normally he teases me about double locking.

ME: to Paige, Jennifer and Theresa; he thinks they are filming a porno at the other end of the hotel. Lol we are doing under cover surveillance. They have had 2 food deliveries in the last hour.

PAIGE: Ha Ha too funny

ME: I think he's board, currently eating popcorn with the curtains barely open

PAIGE: OMG dad is bored!!

JENNIFER: What hotel does dad bring you to?? lol

ME: yep. I just thought we needed someone to tell the police why we were killed :)

THERESA: a promo, for what??

JENNIFER: just cheeching it up mom, that's all :)

PAIGE: my co-workers think the porn film is just high and hungry kids

ME: to Theresa; no, porno, not promo

ME: to everyone; there is a red light shining through the curtains.

THERESA: OMG are you hearing something.

PAIGE: Jennifer thinks dad is having SOA withdrawal

JENNIFER: I think dad is having Sons of Anarchy withdrawal.

ME: to Theresa; No it's across the parking lot

JENNIFER: well don't you have lights in your room

JENNIFER: mom, how dare you questions dad's knowledge of porn. OMG LOL

ME: to Paige; could be. But dad said he saw someone take a light on a pole from one room to the one next door. And what about the pink feather uh???

PAIGE: lol

ME: to Jennifer; not red lights!!

JENNIFER: is dad going to ask if they need help holding the lights lol

ME: to Paige, Jennifer and Theresa; plus there was a guy with dreadlocks going between the two rooms.

THERESA: see if they need any extras. Does Will want you to borrow the pole. You can belly dance / pole dance. LOL

ME: to Paige and Jennifer; dad just saw a guy carry an empty brown bag into one room and little bit later he came out with stuff in the bag.

ME: to Theresa; LOL belly dance, Yes, pole dance, No

ME: to everyone; well I do have pictures, and just FYI you cannot look up a license plate online.

JENNIFER: dread locks mean cheech not porn, mom!!

ME: to everyone; what about the car he saw last night with the hula hoops. I told him they might have been here for a cheer-leading thing. Looked on line and didn't see anything. He says they were not cheer-leading hula hoops. They were porn hula hoops..???

PAIGE: HAHA OMG

JENNIFER: could be drugs

PAIGE: They know ho's usually aren't the healthiest people unless it's a Cinemax porn and they always talk too much anyways. That's what I have been told I never seen one thou...lol

ME: well now dad thinks it's all drugs, closed the curtains. Said been there done that, and won't let me take any more pictures, says that's serious shit

THERESA: LOL

ME: well all that excitement wore out the ol' man, nap time. He told me to leave the curtains alone

PAIGE: Are you going to blog this

Around 3am Will got up and looked out the window to see what was making noise and he saw a girl wearing daisy dukes and a guy stumble into a room, clue # oh who cares.

The next day when we check out there are two housekeepers in the lobby dividing up the rooms to be cleaned. The clerk tells them room 112 is leaving.

One housekeeper said, what number, Oh ok. Boy I hope that other room doesn't leave today. The other housekeeper says which one? "You know which one"
"Ah ha, lordy yes, I'm off tomorrow let Timlinda clean it. Awa-ha. She can do that".
Then they both giggle. And shake their heads.

Well there you go. Do we need to contact Leonard Nimoy and tell him there are more unsolved mysteries in Memphis besides if James Earl Ray acted alone?

Should we let Timlinda know that her co-workers think she has exceptional housekeeping skills?

And most importantly, do we really want to know what Will thinks porn hula hoops look like?

I love and miss you all

Oregon vs. the rest of the States

Since I'm not getting lost, Probably due to my daily novenas to Saint Christopher, patron saint of travelers and Saint Anthony, patron saint of lost things, I am running out of 'lost stories'

While traveling around this country, I have decided we need to make some changes. Not big changes just obvious ones. But if I were Dictator...

First, there are a few states we don't need anymore, actually not sure why we needed them to begin with. Wyoming, Nebraska, Kansas and Iowa, sorry your out 'a here. You're too windy to keep. Calm down people, we can import their beef and corn. We will even be willing to pay more for them because they are "imported". That should improve their local economies.

Well Kansas City has a great Irish Heritage Center so guess we will keep Kansas, but you're on notice.

I think we should keep Idaho and Montana, get rid of anything east of Missoula. Boise State has a heck of a football team. We need to keep Clinton Montana; the Rock Creek Lodge has the Testicle Festival. (Just saying it makes me giggle)

I don't see any reason to keep North Dakota, well wait that's where Fargo is, and that was a good movie, aww gezz. We should keep South Dakota just because of the cool towns, Deadwood, Sturgis, Spearfish. Spearfish? Sure you know Spearfish. The Spearfish Creek is unusual because it's one of the few rivers that freeze from the bottom up. I hear it's a great place to go fishing in the middle of winter.

Wisconsin we have to keep just for all the great cheese.

Texas, start packing. Don't tell me you haven't thought about it too. It is too hot. The roads are awful. Yes I did sign the on line petition to let Texas Secede.  They think they are too good to be part of the United States anyway. The Texas state flag is flown everywhere, but not always alongside the US flag. Let them be their own country, so giddy up and giddy out. Oh and take Oklahoma with you. We will, of course, have to arrange a secret covert operation to extract ZZ Top and Willie Nelson for purely selfish reasons.

Ok what's left?

Well Tennessee we have to keep. We spend a lot of time off in Memphis. I Love Beale Street.

Will says we have to keep New Jersey otherwise there would be no Sopranos. But I think we have to let the shore side go, for the greater good of course.

Arizona. Is the prospect of standing on a corner in Winslow Arizona worth keep an entire state? NO, sorry Arizona, you are way too HOT and your dust storms are un real.

 They have to put this sign up because yes, people just stop in the middle of the road during a dust storm.

I think the rest we can keep. They have enough trees to make me happy even if some of their summer temperature and humidity are too high for me

There are a lot of things we don't normally see in Oregon. I'll start with the obvious thing you don't see much of in Oregon. The Sun. Lebanon, on average gets about 50" of rain a year. About 2" of snow. And about 68 days without rain. Our average winter temp about 37' and average summer temp is about 78'. We don't have devastating tornados. We don't worry about earthquakes when we're on a bridge or overpass. We worry about making it across before a bridge lift, during fleet week.

We don't have weird bugs or snakes. Well there is an ongoing debate over the brown recluse spider. Will calls it a Fiddle Back spider. Experts say it doesn't live here, but everybody that has a wood pile, has a story about one. Our forest actually has trees, unlike Wyoming.

You won't find orange trees ripe in January.. You won't find standalone ~ self-service, ice machines

Things you CAN see in Oregon. Free beach access!!!

Since the 1960's Oregon as had a law that in short says private landowners cannot restrict the public's access to the beach. There are only a couple of beaches where you can still drive onto the sand but other than that, if you can find a place to park you can walk to the beach. FYI Hawaii is the only other state that guarantees the public has free and uninterrupted use and access to beaches. The water is a lot warmer and more inviting there. OH Heck yeah we're keeping Hawaii, might even get to visit it

If you're lucky you can see snow on the Oregon Beach. A rare site, but very cool. You can see bald eagles flying over Hwy 34, just about 5 miles from our house. You don't have to pump your own gas. In fact you are not allowed.

We have the Oregon Country Fair. (Ok maybe not one of our proudest but a very popular event) They say they discourage drug use, but I heard gates open at 4:20. Some of you might get the significance of that ~ and if you do shame, shame on you.

At Silver Creek Falls, there are falls you can walk behind, that's cool!

You can find the BEST POPCORN in the world here. Joe Brown Carmel Corn. Yes, you can order on line, No they don't pay me.

You will find an intense yet friendly, web footed rivalry between Ducks and Beavers. Many families, (as is ours) are divided by a green vs. orange line. I guess I am big enough to give credit where credit is due, Congratulations Ducks for not embarrassing the state at the Rose Bowl, like you have before.

Even with my Irish blood,
I BLEED ORANGE......GO BEAV'S

The best thing about Oregon is this.

If you're lucky you can attend my grandkids jam session.   Love and miss you

Our Youngest Graduates

As you know our son was left home when we started this adventure. A senior in high school. Living most teenage boys dream. Months with no parental supervision. Most parents would not have left, some would have left and not come back. But our son probably did not even know we were gone for a couple of months. I freeze single servings of left overs every time we are home. All he has to do is pop it in the microwave. He spends all his time on his computer, in school, at the Magic the Gathering card store and with the robotics team.

In fact the most trouble he got in was when one of our daughters wanted to use our living room for a pampered chef party. She cleaned and got everything ready the day before so when she got off work she would already be set up for her party. The timing of her party was bad. It happened to be on the same weekend as a Star Wars marathon. And according to our daughter, "He invited all his geeky, stinky friends over and used silly string as light sabers and messed up the whole house, at 3pm they were still sleeping all over the house". I said did you tell him to clean up his mess? Yes. Did he clean up his mess? Yes. Then what's the problem?

The graduation was very good. It did rain towards the end of the ceremony, but that didn't dampen anyone's spirits. One neat thing that they did was after calling a student's name to come forward, they also announced what each student's plans were for the future.

90 percent of the seniors announced they were going to continue on to college. If that really happens, then that seems like it would be some sort of record. Some announced they were going in the military. There were some individuals that announced they were going to pursue an acting career, photography, crime scene investigator, become a Congressman or President. And a few actually went with the truth. They announced after leaving high school they plan on joining the work force, or just lying around on their mothers couch. A couple others simply announced they were 'going to get on with their lives'. I think those students got the most applause from people they didn't know. When they got to our son he announced he was planning to attend Oregon State University and pursue a career in Engineering. I was thinking, how glad I was that, they did not do that for my high school graduation.

"*After graduation Leslie has decided not to pursue her dream job as a paralegal, instead she plans on marrying her longtime, drug addicted boyfriend, hoping to change him. After an abusive year, they will divorce, leaving Leslie a single teenage mother. Having honed her enabling skills on her first marriage, she again forgoes a paralegal education and plans on marring hoping to change him.....*"

We are on our way to Ohio with Kingsford charcoal from Springfield. I can't believe that a truck full of charcoal is not hazmat. Isn't it combustible, shouldn't it be kept away from flames? It's also funny that a load of fire extinguishers is considered a Haz-Mat load. It's a heavy load 44,000 we are just barely able to take it. Lucky it is heavy in the right places, so

~ 164 ~

Will can adjust the rear axles. Our fuel mileage is going to suffer. This is not a team load. It may be 2500 miles but we have 6 days to get there. We asked our DM if we could deliver it early, it will only take us 3 days. She said she would ask the customer service rep on this account and find out. That was Thursday, today is Friday and she is not in today. We sent a message asking if we were able to drop this early and our response was, "Your DM is not in today". Well can't the person taking her place find out for us? NO! Guess not.

It's hard to believe that the load planners actually plan loads. I think they just pull the next one available out of a hat, and give it to the next truck on their list. If the *load planners, planned* this load they should have *planned* on a team getting the load to delivery in half the time it takes a solo driver. They should have *planned* on us either delivering it early or dropping the trailer somewhere and issue us another load. I think they should take the "planner" part out of their job description. They are just giving us a load. Their title should be load givers.

The weather this trip has just been awful. Wyoming started it all. The down pouring of rain, oh my gosh. Then I80 took us into Nebraska and they threw in more wind than in Wyoming, and lightening and more rain. It was like driving through Niagara Falls. It was so bad that Will pulled over and we sat for a few hours until the wind became more reasonable. Gee wasn't I just complaining about a load that was too heavy. Funny how things work out. There are only a few times I wish for a heavy load, and they are snow and wind. Will said if we had one of those 7000 pound loads that I like we wouldn't have made it this far. We would have to stop in Wyoming for a few hours. In Illinois and Indiana the rain came and went, but there was also lightening. We will be there early Sunday but we cannot delivery until Tuesday afternoon. No Money, no money, no money. ugh!! I am already counting the days to our next home time.

Love and miss you all, already

Rain, Rain Go Away

After butting heads with our DM, we tested her advice saying we have the right to turn down loads we do not want without load planner retaliation. We turned down one load because it was short miles. We turned down a second load because it also was low miles. After turning down the second load our pta was changed. PTA is projected time available, when you tell the load planners you will be ready to drive again. If we set our pta at 0600, and a load planner changes it to 2359 that means we are sitting about 18 hours before someone will start looking for a load for us.   Luckily our DM was still in. I sent her a message, ok a sarcastic message. 'Well will you look at that, somehow our pta changed. Now I know nobody is allowed to change our pta as a form of retaliation for turning down loads so there must e a glitch in the system, could you reset our pta, please and thank you'

A little while later a load planner sent us a message asking if we could 'do a favor' and deliver a load, the other driver ran out of hours. The load is in Lake Charles and the load planner promised to back it up with a load that had miles. I asked to see the backup load. Last time a planner sent us to Atlanta saying they had a good back up load, they gave us 650 miles to Lake Charles. They sent the load, Lake Charles to Phoenix. 1800 miles.

So now it was our turn to pull a fast one on them. Well actually it was Will's idea. The favor they wanted us to do would take hours off our logs, fuel out of our truck and just add to our frustration level because it was a live unload. Since it was passed the delivery time, most company's make you wait until they have time or until the next driver shows up late, then we can have their dock time. It was only about 10 miles away. We would make no money doing this favor in fact it would mean we would not have the hours to do the backup load they sent.

So, after they sent us the preplan for both loads. We declined the favor load and accepted the backup load to Phoenix. Boy, were they mad at us. The load planner said we must take both loads. We explained that the hours did not work out, we cannot do both. As owner ops, we have a choice! Again they said we need to do both, we can't do one without doing the other. The load planner said if we take the favor load it will benefit us in the future, next time we are in this area and need a good load they will help us.

~ 167 ~

We told her next time we are in this area they will know who to screw and get free work out of. We told her there were 4 company drivers in the lounge complaining of no loads, give it to one of them.

She said if we take the favor load we won't have to look for an empty trailer. Are they insane? We came in to the yard with an empty, I told her that, and that we are still attached to it. We want our info for the Phoenix load. Will made it clear it was not legal for White Trucking to ask us to do some work for free in exchange for a team load. Did they need us to confirm our opinion with Mr. C.O.O (He who I cannot name without permission.) of White Trucking? He has been very helpful in the past. He actually takes our concerns seriously. He does not consider us whinny drivers. He does not talk down to us. He does not treat us as stupid drivers that can be replaced. (And dropping his name a couple of times a year seems to help) So they sent our info.

I guess this whole thing could play out one of two ways, they could say, well we can't pull anything over on those drivers, they're too smart for us. Which I doubt, or they may say, screw them, they want to play games then game on.

Now we are headed to Phoenix from Louisiana with a trailer full of tires for the White Trucking yard. We picked up the tires at the Bridgestone Firestone factory. Leaving rush hour in any city is always an adventure. Friday just makes is more interesting. Add rain and it just doesn't get any better than that. Why is it called rush hour, there is no rush and it lasts more than an hour?

Leaving Lake Charles Louisiana, there are a couple of really cool bridges that go over swamps, bayous and plain old lakes. There is a bridge, is a long two lane low to the water bridge. There are two sides of travel.

2 lanes going west and another bridge with 2 lanes going east. The truck speed is 55 and we have to stay in the right lane. No passing. It is called Atchafalaya Basin Bridge. The bridge is 18.2 miles long. It is the tenth longest bridge in the world by total length. Accidents occur frequently near the two river crossings as both are very narrow and lack shoulders. And I thought you would like to know the Atchafalaya Basin, or Atchafalaya Swamp, is the largest swamp in the United States.

I also had to look up the difference between swamp and bayou. Parts of this bridge cross, Henderson Bayou and Atchafalaya Swamp. Here is what I found out.

A bayou is a very slow-moving stream, attached to a larger stream or river, and usually with many open spaces. Swamps are full of vegetation with few wide open places like bayous.

In Louisiana and Mississippi, it is the Mississippi River that feeds bayous and swamps. While a bayou is usually an open stream with vegetation along the sides, a swamp is a boggy wetland where water seems to stand still, although its water does rise and fall with freshwater tides.
The other bridge looks more like a roller coaster.

The steep bridge is over the Calcasieu River, just west of Lake Charles.

We are taking our 34 hours off before we get into Phoenix, that way we will be able to start the week fresh with 70 hours each to work. Can't wait for to see what happens next week.

Love and miss you all.

Chicago, no Oprah Sighting

Well, life goes on. We got a load to Chicago, everything went fine. Good miles and it was a good trip. We even got a reload right away. It didn't pick up until 10pm local time. So we went to a truck stop where you can stay for 3 hours for free after that is cost $10. We made sure to leave after 2 hours and 45 min. We went to the pickup location and the driver that talked to us could not have had a more Chicago accent if he tried. We asked where he wanted us to put our empty trailer. He said, "Remember where I told's youz ta put it last time" I said no this is our first time here.

'O O yea right, paak it down theres by the brown door ya load won't be ready tills 11'
I hope when you read that you were using your Elwood from Blues Brothers voice, only thicker.

We comes back at 10:30 and they say the load is ready but they need a pickup number from us to confirm we are who we are and we are taking the right load.

So's anyway, back to my story. We contact White Trucking and tell them we need a pickup number. They said the load isn't ready yet, they will give us the number when ready. We told them it is ready and we are sitting under it and hooked up to it, need the pickup number so's we can get the paperwork and leave. We can't leave until 'we gives the guy the secret code' (it was late and we were having fun at someone else's expense. sorry karma) So's after 1 and 1/2 hours White Trucking sends us the secret pickup code. So much for being early.

Will gives it to the guy, and asks the guy why it was loaded the way it was, all the weight appeared to be in the back of the trailer. We will have to move the tandem axles to California requirements. He says don't worry he loads them this way all the time. We head off to the scale 20 miles away. 20 miles thru Chicago is 45 minutes. It doesn't surprise Will that it is too heavy and we cannot adjust the axles to move the weight. We send White Trucking a message that we have to go back and have the load adjusted. They said ok keep them informed. We get back there and the business is closed. Have to wait until morning.

That disturbance in the force you felt was Will's head exploding.

I sent a message, saying shipper closed for the day, have to wait until morning. I also asked if we were going to be getting detention pay, if we were not then we want another load and we will leave this one here. They said don't worry we will get detention pay. I took a picture of that message from them. Taking a picture of the messages is the only proof we have of she said he said sort of thing. The messages drop off after about 50 messages.

In the morning the day shift was gripping about having to redo the load he said he wanted to wait until the evening shift came in and make them re-do it. Eventually someone talked to someone and we were reloaded. When we left to go scale again, I sent a message telling them we were going to scale again and asked if our detention pay continues until we have a legal load. And they sent back a message saying yes. I took a picture of that to. After all that now it is my turn to drive and we are still in Chicago. Will wasted his whole 14 hour shift getting scaled and then waiting until morning. In our short time in Chicago, I did not see Oprah. I did see the exit for Joliet. "I hear they have a wicked pepper steak, but not as bad as the oatmeal at the Cook County slammer". Hope you got that Blues Brothers reference, one of my all-time favorite movies.

We make our way to Mira Loma in an uneventful trip. We have a reload already too. We pick up a FedEx load in San Bernardino, CA and take it to Boise, Idaho. We've picked up FedEx here before they are pretty good about being on time. Our route takes us thru Nevada, hope to win big.

After we get to Idaho, our DM tells us that we are only getting 10 hours detention pay! That is the most they pay. I told her after 10 hours they should have sent us another load. Next time I'm leaving.

I HATE THIS JOB

Love and miss you all

Trucker Talk

This is my new language I thought you might find interesting. Truck drivers will try to get your attention by calling you by whoever you are working for. Like "Hey White Trucking", "Hey Warner". If they can't see or read your company name they'll use the color and make of your truck. "Hey black Pete", "Hey blue KW". Most of the time the other drivers are nice to me. There are lots of times when there is something going on in front of me and I want to change lanes the truck behind me will say, "Come on in miss White Trucking" letting me get in front of him to avoid the problem. The older drivers I think were nicer than the younger ones. The younger guys felt like this is their job, this is a man's job and they were just always full of piss and vinegar. The older guys figure everyone needs a job and just do your job correctly and safely and don't slow them down.

Here is some of the CB lingo.

Break check… slow down, stopped traffic ahead:

Back it down…slow down, lower your speed

4 wheelers… cars

Lot lizard or commercial company…truck stop hooker

Chicken coop...weigh station: the opposite direction will ask about it. North bound drivers will ask south bound side if the coop is open, or the opposite direction will warn other drivers it's open.

Creeper at the coop...weigh station is open and doing vehicle inspections

Seat cover... a good looking female driver

Evel Knievel... motorcycle cop

Barney...local police

Bear or Smokey... Highway patrol, a diesel bear is a DOT cop

With a customer ... police have someone pulled over

Taking pictures...police with a radar gun

Meat wagon/ Band aid box...ambulance

Gator...blow out tire rubber on the road

Got your ears on?...Is your CB radio turned on?

Back door...behind you: drivers will ask the opposite side of drivers "what da' leave at your back door?" mostly wanting a traffic report, police report, weather report etc.

Super trucker...semi that is speeding or driving unsafe.

Travel agent...your dispatcher

Wheels up...a vehicle upside down. "north bound you got a 4 wheeler, wheels up at the 234 yard stick"

Litter Box / Sand Box...the gravel area trucks use when they lose their breaks going downhill. "East side litter box is full" some drivers give the driver in the litter box a bad time.

Dragonfly...a truck that drags up the hill and fly's down the hill: some drivers warn other drivers they're truck is a dragonfly, then they can go around you, lets them know you are going to be going slow

Come back... waiting for an answer: "hey there White Trucking you got your ears on, come back"

Barefeet...when you don't have to put on chains for snow or ice: "Bare feet at the pass"

Throw iron, or put you jewelry on...put on chains. Depends on your truck, log trucks, flat beds would throw iron. A nicely painted truck or one with a lot of chrome, or I would hear, "hey Miss White, you'll need your jewelry at the pass".

Bumper Sticker...A car driving to close to your rear bumper. That extra piece of metal that has reflector tape on it, that is called a D.O.T bumper. Know why it's there? Too many cars drive too close to a semi's bumper, thinking they are getting better gas mileage by drafting. Too many cars end up under the trailer when the truck has to stop or slow down. The bumper was specifically added to help reduce the number of deaths caused by vehicles crashing into the back of the semi. First, how do you not see a semi, second, stop driving like an idiot.

And tons more, but most of it you can just figure out. Like if I am going south and a truck in the north bound wants to talk to me they might say. 'South bound White you got a black eye, and your coop is open. He's telling me I have a head light out I should fix because the next weigh station ahead of me is open
'East bounders you got a Barney takin' pictures at the 137' they are saying there is a cop with a radar gun at the 137 mile marker.
'West bound, back it down, break check, break check, got 2 four wheelers fighting over the same piece of real estate' That's telling us to slow down, there is a 2 car accident ahead'
"Red Pete, in back row looking for commercial company, come back"
That's a driver in a red Peterbuilt, asking for a hooker.

I can't wait till my travel agent can get a layover at my home 20

Love and miss you all

America the Beautiful

It certainly is a Beautiful country we live in. The ever green trees in the northwest smell great. The changing leaf colors on the east coast are such a nice change for me. Moab, Utah is a beautiful place. The different shades of red in the rocks are breathtaking. Wilson's Arch is such a sight. The amber waves of grain are something I wish everyone could see. But maybe the song should be changed to rows of corn. I do not think this country will run out of corn. The churches and barns in the mid-west really take you back in time. I love seeing the old rock and stone churches with big steeples, even the little ones tucked into a small town are great to catch a sight of.

Love and miss you all

Guess who got a ticket

No it wasn't Will. It was me...ME? ME!!!!

I know, I can't believe it either. Now I admit I could have been day dreaming, thinking about my high school having to get rid of its mascot because it is offensive to Indians. Like the Lebanon Warriors.

I like to think things out and take them to their obvious illogical conclusion. Will we have to change names like Milwaukee, which is Algonquian and means a good place? Massachusetts, from the Massachusett tribe, which means 'a great hill'.

What about the rebels or the pirate's? Do we really want our kids trying to live up to the values of a pirate?

I wonder how much it cost Lake Tahoe to keep the name Squaw Valley. How long is it before the ASPCA tells us we can't have mascots like, The Bull Dogs, or The Raven's? Did Los Angles get permission from God to be called the City of Angles? Did Saint Francis give a nod of approval to San Francisco? What about Hawaii State University, they are the Warriors.

Or I could have been thinking about the new suggested law that says truck drivers cannot use hands free communication devices. Now I understand the reason behind not texting while you drive. Believe me I know, because it is much harder to text and drive with my new phone. But the reason behind wanting to ban hands free is because law makers are saying you are still distracted while talking on your blue tooth. Well then, they should also put a muzzle on all your passengers in case you are tempted to have a conversation. They should take away the radio so you're not tempted to sing. Don't forget eating while driving. It takes one hand to eat so both your hands are not on the wheel, and don't you always glance down to make sure you are aiming your cup towards the cup holder. Take out all the GPS's I know you look at the screen to make sure you are taking the correct exit.

And don't think of what is going on at home. Don't think about missing your grand-daughters first parade or their ballet recital. Don't think about how much fun you had last time you took your grandson to the zoo

But back to my ticket, I still can't believe it. Just 3 days ago I was the toast of Mississippi, passed my D.O.T inspection got a "Thank you and have a safe trip" from the officer. He should have added stay the hell out of Texas.

We were picking up a load in Lubbock Texas (YEP, I thought you would guess Texas). It's potato chips going to Salt Lake City. The route they sent us was high altitude. White Trucking said they would send us a low altitude route. Have to stay under 6000 feet; otherwise the bags might pop open.

When the new route arrived it was still high altitude so I contacted our manager again. She said she would look into it, but we could take off and she would get ahold of us before we got too high. (In altitude people, for cryin' out loud).

When she finally sent me the new, new route I looked at it and it said I should start on I27 S, but the first set of directions said I27 N. I had to pull over and ask her if she wanted me to turn around and start all over. It was easier to ask her than to wake up Will. She said no the road I'm on will connect with the road I want then all will be good.

I was cruising along in Texas, (somebody make me evil overlord so I can kick Texas out) following my directions, not getting lost. And I saw the flashing lights on the sign that said 'All commercial trucks proceed to scale'. Normally the next sign you see is a big Green one with an arrow that says Scale. Well they didn't have one. I looked over to my right and saw a building that said justice court? Crap.

Well of course, how convenient get a ticket, see the judge and pay the fine all in one quick stop. Less than half a mile later a sheriff of Hale County Texas was pulling me over. He took my license and said "Follow me ma'am".

Yup, it was just like Smokey and the Bandit.

As I was following him back I thought to myself, too bad the roads are so awful, I'd like to put on eye liner, shave my legs etc. I should have put on a different shirt.....where's that Victoria Secret bra Will likes.

Crap..........Crap........Crap.

I was not the only one escorted back to the scales. While I was there another wayward driver also received a personal invitation to the scales. So I think it's a set up. That's my story and I'm sticking to it.

They pulled me into the inspection pit. I gave the officer my D.O.T. medical card that shows I am physically approved to drive. The Bill of Lading, which shows what we are carrying where we got it from. When we picked it up and where we are going. They will be figuring my travel time to determine if I could have arrived here at this time, driving the speed limit. I gave them the permit book for the truck, that includes the license, registration and insurance for the truck. It also includes any special permits we might need for different states, like alcohol or haz-mat. The officer asked if I'd ever been through a Level I inspection before and I said yes, mostly in California.

He said "Well we're not that bad".

That's funny Big Hoss, that's what they say about Texas.

Scarred you uh? You thought I said that out loud, but I used my inside voice.

They did a complete inspection on the truck and trailer. The truck passed with a warning, our fire extinguisher was not secure. The clip came un-clipped. Big Whoop. The trailer got a warning that tires needed to be replaced and signed off on in 15 days. And I got a ticket for failure to comply with a traffic control device. **$200.** "You can pay inside ma'am".

The money hurts but how many points did this screw up just cost me on my license? I bet if I went into the scale, like I was supposed to the tires on the trailer would have passed. But since they didn't I get deducted points for that too.

I told my DM, (not dungeon master, driver manager) that it was my first ticket ever. But I was quickly corrected by someone who loves me very much, or claims he does anyway.

"Not-aw, 10 years ago you got a ticket for running a yellow light on Main Street with a cop already stopped in the lane next to you". Well it didn't seem right for me to slam on the brakes just to end up stopped in the intersection. The ticket said I ran a red light, when I reminded him it was yellow when I went through it 'you were sitting right next to me' he said red and yellow are treated the same.

I said then why do we even have a yellow light?
Why doesn't it just go from green to red. And
since they are the same what difference would it
make if you, just say I ran a yellow light. It was
at that moment I realized that our local Officer
Barney was born without a funny bone.

So that's my M.O. I've got a record.
With priors for ignoring lights and signs.
Continuing to endanger the public with blatant
disregard for laws.

I need to take this opportunity to
apologize to everyone I have let down.

Will asked if I wanted him to write
down where all the scales are. I said that would
be great, but better would be if he could route
me around the scales. He said looks like I can do
that by myself.

Maybe White Trucking should cut their
losses now, before I further disparage the title of
truck driver.

Currently saying a prayer to Saint
Johnny Paycheck. The patron saint of the
willfully unemployed. Some of you may not
know his hit song, "Take this job and shove it".

I admit I thought about what would
happen if I didn't pay. I would have to stop
being a truck driver. Bummer. I would get a
mini vacation, albeit in Texas. But hey, 3 hots
and a cot courtesy of the Grey Bar Inn. I could
end up with another tattoo, (not that I got my
first one in jail) but Will won't let me get another
tramp stamp.

I asked Will if he would come visit me. First he said in TEXAS? Then he got this big smile and his eyes glazed over thinking about possible lesbian encounters, shower scenes, and congeal visits.

**Note to self, buy more lottery tickets.

I love and miss you all so much.

Gomer and Goober are alive and well and living in Georgia

It was bound to happen. Even though I did not hear banjos, we knew exactly where we were.

I got a flat and pulled in to a rest stop on I 16 somewhere south or east of Dublin, Georgia. We called White Trucking, and they sent out road service. They don't actually send out a White Trucking truck, they contact and send out an approved vender that accepts payment from White Trucking. White Trucking will send them the money, take it out of our weekly settlement check and add a $35 charge, for the convenience of having White Trucking do all the phone calling and paper work. That is outrageous. Normally we look on line and make arraignments ourselves or pull into a truck stop for any maintenance or work that needs to be done. That way we can pay cash and save the $35 charge. But sometimes the internet lets us down. It could not come up with any road service companies in the area. (Maybe because we were out in banjo land)

We had to wait 2 ½ hours after White Trucking called us back and told us someone was coming. Good thing we have a lot of time on this load. They came in a small utility truck. Not a real tire truck. Oh sure, they had everything to change a tire. A replacement tire, we hoped it was the right size, an air compressor, and a tool box. I personally think Gomer had already started taste testing this week's batch of moonshine. They discussed their options, quickly surveyed the problem, (quickly is a loose, southern term), and decided they needed to change our tire.

They talked to Will, asking what he was hauling, where he was going, how long he had been a truck driver. Then I got out of the truck to go in and use the restroom, they both stopped. Goober says I see you got a trainee. Will says no that's my wife. (I swear I heard 'Well Gooolly') Gomer asked how that was working out, how long we have been married, how long have we been driving, how often we get home, etc. These guys must think they are getting paid by the hour not by the service call, because they cannot talk, listen and work at the same time. They can however, talk, smoke, chew and spit at the same time.

Normally it takes about 15-20 min, if that long, to change a truck tire. The longest time is waiting for road service to show up. Once they arrive you can start getting stuff ready to roll again. About 10 min after they arrived, I had dinner all set up and told Will it was ready. I love crock pot liners, no mess to clean up and close enough to home cooking. The chili has been cooking most of the day. Chili and chips for dinner. When he got back in the truck and I told him I was going to run to the bathroom before we take off, so don't leave without me. He said no chance of that, they still don't have the tire off the rim.

According to my expert co driver, truck tires used to be very dangerous. You used to have to have a tire cage in order to air up the tire. They were called split rims. If the tire didn't bead right on the split rim then the rim ring would come flying off and take your head off. The rim might explode and send shrapnel everywhere. Will said in the army, back in the day, you just throw the tire under the truck and air it up. Some garages would not even change semi tires because of the danger. Now the tires are tubeless and you don't need any more tools than are required to change a car tire. A jack, a bar, an air wrench and an air compressor. And if the tire is an outside tire you don't even need a jack, just a block of wood.

This is the story Will retells me. They took the rim off the truck and they did not need to. It was an outside tire. Then they started using bars to separate the tire from the rim. They were using bars, the tire was up against the bead. They should have moved the bead to the center of the rim and then the rim pretty much falls right off. While Gomer was man handling 5 bars and 4 vise grips, Goober was in charge of the sledge hammer.

Forty-Five minutes later the tire was lying in the parking lot with the rim still attached. They took a 10 min break. After their progress meeting they decided the problem was they needed more grease. So now there is grease everywhere. Just by luck when they took the bars out to reposition them, the tire fell to the center and they could get it off.

High 5's all around. Aunt Bea must surely be proud. If it wasn't for the entertainment factor Will would have killed them an hour and a half ago. He did tell them to take the vise grips off because he didn't want our custom rims scratched.

Will kept coming in throughout the evening, giving me updates. Laughing and shaking his head.

I wanted to write on the bathroom wall, for a good time call Gomer and Goober. I told Will at least we got dinner and a show out of this flat tire.

And just like that, we are off to deliver in Savannah, Georgia. Oh then to top it off when we signed the invoice they added wrong. They were charging us $132 too much. It's not their fault, it's the new math that's confusing.

Love and miss y'all.

Kentucky

So its 1am in Kentucky and we are stopped at a truck stop, some guy knocks on the driver's side door. Will rolls down the window and the guy starts telling us this story.

"You see those police over there? They are here for your protection. I'm a truck driver too. I just got home from being on the road 3 months. I bust my ass and get home 3 days early and catch my whore of a girlfriend with the neighbor. In my house, in my bed, with my daughter in the house. I have custody of my daughter. I called the cops to kick her out and they said they can't make her leave it's her house too. That's bull shit. So I tell the cops I will take my daughter and leave. They tell me if I don't have a safe place to take my daughter they won't let me take her to sleep in my truck. They'll have to call emergency foster care. I can't let that happen, please don't let that happen. So she is over there in that patrol car and the cop said they would give me 15 minutes to get enough for a motel room. So I'm here to sell the clothes in my laundry bag, sorry they are dirty man, but I wasn't home long enough to wash them. Or anything else you want from my truck. Tell me want you want and you can have it. Please anything will help."

Well that was either the truth or the best begging for money story Will ever heard, so he gave him a $50.

Love and miss you all

Nothing to do but Complain.

How can one State and one terminal cause me so much heart burn? Yes you guessed it, Texas. Our last trip was to Amarillo.
We were scheduled to pick up a load weighing 35000 lbs, going to Laredo. Not really good miles, but from Laredo we usually get a GM load to Detroit. When we arrive, we check in, drop the empty, continue to shipping department to sign in, go find and hook to our preloaded trailer. Will said it didn't feel right. We stop at shipping on the way out to sign and receive our paperwork only to find out the actual weight is 45,000. Too heavy for us. We told the shipping clerk, he shook his head and says happens all the time. A lot of White Trucking drivers come in expecting a lower weight. He said all the shipments weigh this amount. So we had to do all that in reverse.

We (I) contacted White Trucking telling (yelling) our frustration and deciding to take our 34 off in Amarillo.

We ate at the 'World Famous' Big Texan Steak house. They offer a FREE STEAK DINNER all you have to do is eat the 72oz steak in 1-hour. You pay for it first, $75, then if you finish you get your money back and your name on a plaque. While we were there, a man was attempting this feat. There is a live camera where you can watch too. It is at bigtexan.com

He did not finish, but received a round of applause from the restaurant goers for his effort.

   They also have a shooting gallery where you can wait for your table. I shot a rifle and Will picked a pistol. He shot better than me. He must have cheated. Will had a 12oz steak and I had 8oz steak. Not a lot of chicken choices. They also offer free Cadillac ride from your hotel to the restaurant, we did not know this and had to drive the semi. Not to bad, they have big truck parking.

The next day after resetting our hours and receiving only one short mile load, we tell dispatch that since there are no team loads here we will relocate ourselves to Oklahoma City. A Funny thing happened on the way to Oklahoma. After complaining about only receiving solo loads we were told we were not listed as a team in the system and to get with our Driver Manager on Monday to correct it.

Well of course I was furious. My fingers could not keep up with my range. I sent a message on the qualcom. I posted on White Trucking's Facebook page asking how after 3 years we are suddenly not a team. (Has it only been 3 years seems like a life time)

On Monday our dm fixes the problem. But that doesn't fix my anger. I sent an e-mail to the Lancaster, Texas terminal manager, asking how this happened. His reply was the 11 solo hours his load planner saw was correct and suggested we make sure we are on the correct driving line on our logs. We have electronic logs! It is hard not to be on the correct line. Every morning we send in a driver status report. That shows our eta to the next stop and our pta, projected time available. We reported that on July 7 our pta would be 22hrs. They want teams to have a minimum of 22 hours available. On July 8, after not driving, we still had a pta of at least 22 hours.

So I sent a second email to our terminal manager, the Lancaster, Texas terminal manager and because I had time, to the COO of White Trucking. My question to Lancaster was how the system can show we only had 11 solo hours available when I reported over 22 team hours

~ 191 ~

available. His second email included (selected) screen shots, which proved his point. There is a program running in the back ground that projects our pta. He called it a virtual pta (not sure why we have to put in a reality pta then) The screen shots were interesting in what they showed and didn't show. He showed a screen shot of our driver status on July 8 that showed we had 22 hrs. And a screen shot of July 6 that showed we had 11 hrs. Which is true, that's why we took our 34 off on July 6. So I still do not understand if a screen shot on July 8 shows 22 hours available. Why, later, on July 8 a load planner believed us to only have 11 hrs. I think it is a losing argument.

No matter what, we all know what happened. The load planner got pissed off and got an attitude. First when we refused that load in Amarillo, the one that was too heavy and second one when they sent us a low miles load that was also hazmat. That put them in a spot. They argued the miles made it a team load because it was 650 miles but not in time. It did not deliver for 2 ½ days. A solo driver with hazmat could have taken it. In 2 ½ days we are able to drive 1500 miles. The problem is there are not that many hazmat drivers. So we believe the load planner changed our available hours, or choose to only look at the incorrect pta. That later statement was added only as a remote possibility it was not done on purpose.

The response from face book was as expected. Everyone believes that is exactly what happened. Everyone had a different story of how a load planner got back at them for refusing a load.

Our dm said it doesn't benefit them to make us appear to be solo. She said they have a lot of team loads that need to run. I said the only benefit would be the load planner's satisfaction of punishing us. She did not say that the hours were changed on purpose. When I asked her if there were any safe guards on their end to restrict load planners changing our pta, she did not get back to me. So it is possible for the pta I put in to be changed or as she suggested 'corrected'. Too her benefit, she did not try to make excuses for what happened, in fact she said she can't change what happened, while she was gone over the weekend, let's just move on.

I cannot believe how mad I am over this. As you can probably tell because I'm rambling on and on.

Anyway the reason I have time to ramble on and on is because we are sitting in Edwardsville, (Kansas City) without a load. There are a lot of trucks here so that tells us there are not a lot of loads. So it does not appear anyone is picking on us….not this time.

I so hate Texas and truck driving.

Love and Miss you all ......very much.

Will's Mom Passed Away

I'll give credit where credit is due. We were in Wisconsin when we got a call from Will's sister about mom. The hospice nurses thought that her time was getting close. We contacted White Trucking and told them what was going on and we needed to get back home to Oregon ASAP. They got us a preloaded Lowes trailer going right to Lebanon.

Thank you guys.

We made it in time. With the medicine Ruth was on she didn't even know we were there, but being there eased Will's mind.

Ruth did not have an easy life, and she had a strained relationship with some of her kids. But I never had a problem with her. I never had any monster in law issues. In fact when I would complain about Will, my mother would say I should talk with my priest and get marriage counseling. Ruth would say, I don't know why you don't leave him I wouldn't put up with that shit.

We are concerned now about Wills step-dad. He spent years taking care of and doing things for Ruth. There are a lot of things to take care of now. Thankfully Will's sister will handle most of it.

We are thankful that at last Ruth is at peace and no longer in pain.

R.I.P Ruth Ann

Love and miss you all

Big Changes

Stay tuned. We have some big changes coming in the very near future. We have had our fill of White Trucking. There are a lot of different issues, but when you add them all together it is not working for us. Some of it is not White Trucking's fault. Will says some of it is just the way trucking is done now. The way they pay you has changed. When Will started driving you were paid based on the actual miles you drove, called hub miles. Now the pay is based on something called household moving miles. That is not address to address. It is about 50-75 miles shorter. I believe companies are allowed to be off 10% on the amount of miles you drive and what you get paid for, and they are certainly taking advantage of that.

Another reason for a change is because we need to improve our miles. We want and are capable of driving about 6000 miles a week. We do not believe our working relationship with White Trucking is as professional as it should be, and I do take my share of blame on that complaint. While I am thankful for the experience White Trucking has given me I think it is time to make room for another piece of meat in the seat to join the ranks.

Love and miss you all

Hello Orange Trucking

We are starting with a new company. Orange Trucking. Which suits the OSU Beaver Lover in me just fine. Two weeks home was a great reminder of what our goal is, what we are working towards. Being able to spend more time with our family and friends.

After passing another DOT Physical and urine test, Orange Trucking also requires a hair sample drug test. They clipped a good size from the back of my scalp. And since Will doesn't have any hair on his head they had to shave both forearms to get enough for the sample.

The list of items Orange Trucking told us to bring did not include supplies for more than a few days. So Will and I debated about whether or not that meant we would be going home after being issued a truck, or if bringing supplies for more than a week was just expected as common knowledge. So we compromised. Clothes for 1 week and some truck stuff. GPS, laptop.

They had us staying at the Clarion Hotel in Portland. Very nice. But the pool was cold and the hot tub was burning our eyes with the amount of chlorine. I cannot say enough good things about the bed. I tried to steal it but Will wouldn't help me carry it. The physical aptitude testing was not as bad as I thought it was going to be.

More frustrating was the drive test. I had a feeling if I got nervous and started to mess up my backing, the instructor would help me.

That turned out not to be the problem. Shifting was the issue.

My four illustrious years of experience included only an 8 speed transmission. And this truck is a 10 speed. Will said I actually drove a 9 speed but you never use 1st gear.

Will says the truck we are getting is going to be a 10speed. I started my test drive with the caveat I have never driven a 10 speed. The instructor told me not to worry I'd be fine. He also said I'd never driven an 8 speed before but I got used to that didn't I?

Will did his test drive first, no problems of course. After about 10 miles we pulled into a warehouse area and changed drivers. Will explained to me that the gear shifter is sloppy and the rpm's shifting

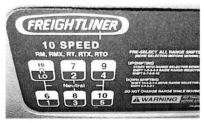

point was a little different. I started off ok, no problems. After trying and grinding and missing and stalling and searching for 6th gear, I decided that there was nothing wrong with driving around Portland in 5th gear.

When we get back to the class room we told the other two new drivers my trouble shifting and one of the guys, the one with as much experience as Will, tells me I don't have to use 1st or 6th gear. I can continue to use the H pattern I'm used to.

He said Just start in 2nd then go to 3rd, 4th, 5th, shift to high then 7th, 8th, 9th, 10th. I looked at Will and he says, Yea, oh yea you can do that. WTH! Thanks Mike. That would have been helpful Will.

I did a great job on my backing. The instructor tells me to just put it back where we got it from, and then got out. Will said I scarred him with my forward driving.   I went about setting myself up to back. Looking at the empty spot, going past till the drive tires just pass it, turn hard right, count to 10 then hard left until I see the spot. Back up, go forward to straighten up, do that a couple more times and just like that I'm in.

The whole time Will is telling me, **you're doing it wrong! Where are you going? What hole are you looking at? Are you even using your mirrors? Your dyslexia is getting worse!**

I told him, Dave is over there having a cigarette maybe you should start smoking, do you want to join him, but by then I was parked. I did not hit a cone, or anything else and I was in my spot. Most importantly I passed and nobody got hurt, (not even Will)

After all that, Orange Trucking does not have a team truck for us yet. Need to give them a day or two to find us one. Teams get a new truck. And right now on the west coast they are all in California.

So we are home for a couple of days re-thinking what we are taking with us. We cannot have an inverter so there will be no refrigerator or microwave. That is going to be hard to get used to. How am I going to keep yogurt and salad? How is Will going to make coffee. It seems contradictory to have trucking companies, tell drivers to stay fit and eat right. But not allow you to have a refrigerator or microwave to help you accomplish that. They are forcing drivers to make poor choices. Truck stop food is not healthy. Even though they have apples and bananas. They all have some fast food joint attached to them or a quick sit down buffet. Paying for every meal, snack, and coffee at fast food prices is incredible expensive.

We will be making some big changes concerning food. Lots of PB&J sandwiches. (Jelly in those restaurant packs, from Costco). Maybe a couple days of yogurt in an ice chest, sandwich meat and cheese, mayo in the packets. But I'm sure it will all work out, we are not the first team and we won't be the last team to live without a refrigerator & microwave.

There is still a lot to learn with Orange Trucking but we can't wait to get started on this new chapter in our team driving adventure. Love and miss you all

Week one with Orange Trucking

They did not have a new truck in the Northwest so they rented us a car and we drove down to Fontana, California. When we get to Fontana, we meet our new driver manager.

~ 199 ~

They do stuff a little different here. They have a driver manager dedicated to only teams. YES! They also have ones assigned to solos, and dedicated routes, also a separate owner operator division with solo and team managers. I think this is where we should have started.

We are just about a week into our new driving adventure with Orange Trucking. We have a brand spanking new 2012 Freightliner Cascadia.

Some things are going to take longer to get used to than others. Like the shifting, OK, Mostly the shifting. It's a 10 speed, just like Will warned me. An 8 speed is just a big **H** shifting pattern just like a car. But on a ten speed, 1st and 6th gear are over to the left and down. (Reverse is over to the left and up). I am always missing 6th gear. When I do find it I then miss 7th and go straight into 9th. By then the rpm's have dropped enough that by the time I find 6th, I need 5th or 4th. That makes the truck shimmy and shake and stutter, and Will is telling me to **down shift, down shift, go back to 6th.** To which I say, DUH don't you think 6th was my goal to begin with. He keeps telling me **6th is around the horn, after 5th go around the horn? WTH** Like when he would try to help me back he says, **now get under it, get under it!** Get what under what?

The paper/computer work is a little different. In orientation Will kept complaining that we did not have to do all this and all that with White Trucking. I said no <u>WE</u> didn't, <u>I</u> did the computer work.
Most of it is the same, just in a different place or in a different order.

Orange Trucking treats us more like an adult. So far, they have the attitude, you're a competent adult, that's why we hired you now go do your job, and how can we help. With White Trucking you had to ask permission and then report what you were doing. With White Trucking when we would have to get fuel, after stopping and putting in the fuel, White Trucking wants you to send a message saying, 'I just put in fuel'. When arriving at a customer or any place that you were going to have to back up to park, or dock, White Trucking wants you to send in a GOAL message. Get Out And Look. White Trucking has a lot of backing accidents and this is one way, they claim to reduce the accidents, by making drivers aware that they were about to back, checking their surroundings. In case you forgot why you put the truck in reverse and turned your flashers on, I guess.

Most drivers already practice GOAL. Will and many drivers never did the GOAL message. I always did, just because I do not have the 30 years' experience as others. Will and other drivers said it was not safe to take your eyes off of the situation and traffic around you, just to send a text message to your boss, telling him what you were going to do. But this way if you had a backing accident and did not send in your GOAL message you could be fired for not following company policy.

You also don't carry a spare tire here. Orange Trucking figures that tires do not just blow for any reason. If you do a good pretrip, stop and check your tires, like you're supposed to, you will see an issue before it becomes a problem. You just take your truck or trailer to a truck stop and get the tire replaced. Well that's what they say anyway, I'll let you know if it works as well in reality as it does in theory. With White Trucking they will run the tire until it blows. We have picked up hazmat loads with very questionable tires, taken them in to White to be changed and they say 'how far are you going?' 'What's the weight?' 'I think it'll be ok, I've seen worse, those aren't that bad'. 'You have your spare with you right?' There is a sign at all the White Trucking exit gates "Do you have your spare?"

The terminals here all have free showers with towels. They have a car you can sign out so you can drive into town to run personal errands. They have free washers and dryers. Most of the terminals have a cafeteria. Oh and the HazMat pay is a lot better. White Trucking gave us $35 total for hauling a HazMat load; Orange Trucking will pay us $50 each. Detention pay sucks here, hope we don't have to use it much.

The navigation is set up different too. With White Trucking we would have to manually input the address and then stop and get fuel on the way. Orange Trucking has all the address already in the system. When we are sent a load we click GO on the navigation and it has the fuel stops and customer addresses already and the system just takes us from here to there. Their computer system, still a Qualcom, has more customer information. Customer hours, if there is long term parking so you can arrive early and if you are allowed deliver earlier than your appointment.

The truck has a Radar System, which,
I'm sure,
will impress
my dad,
Retired CPO
Adams,
Submarines.
And my
baby
brother,

Retired Senior Chief Adams USN. It is called
On Guard, collision safety system. Kind of cool,
kind of annoying. It judges the speed of a
vehicle in front of us and if the vehicle is too
close or is going too slow it beeps, then it
automatically reduces my speed. It does not
detect cross winds, tornados or deer. Unlike
some USN radar systems, there is absolutely no
danger of dolphins or whales beaching
themselves or birds dropping dead in front of
me because of this radar system.

It does not like when cars are merging
and getting close to the side of you. It beeps and
slows me down, not sure if that is a help at that
moment. It also has a hard time knowing the
difference between a slow moving vehicle and a
bridge. Sometimes it sees the bridge as a
stopped vehicle and slams on the brakes, then
because "you" slammed on the brakes the cruise
control is automatically disabled. Sometimes it
slams the brakes on hard enough that the driver
behind us says, "How's that new radar system
working for ya' Orange?" So I guess the
system's quirks are already well known.

The truck also has smart cruise. Predictive cruise control. It looks ahead and see a corner and will automatically decrease your speed then resume speed as you come out of the corner. It looks ahead and sees a hill, judges the hill and increases your speed then just as you crest the top it will reduce your speed. I used to have to get a running start at hills. But this baby does that for me. It was not fun to have the cruise on while going up a hill empty. Because everyone else was going slowly and the radar

system wanted me to slow down because of the slow traffic up head. I just got over one lane and everything was fine. You can turn off the cruise but you cannot turn off the On Guard Radar. The smart cruise is not smart enough to know the difference between a hill and a slight ramp incline. Like when changing freeways. It still speeds up as if it were just a hill. It is not smart enough to know your weight. If you're empty you don't have to speed up to get up a hill, but it does anyway.

We also have a DEF system, diesel exhaust fluid. This system has a separate tank that we need to fill with a different fluid. It helps to keep our engine at a zero emissions. Our International did not have this system. There are 4 bars on the gauge to let you know how full it is. So when we get low on DEF, I tell Will we are at DEF con 1.

My sister thinks I should paper the truck with OSU Beaver stickers. Like I bleed Orange, Powered by Orange, Orange Crush and Beaver Nation. I think she's right, but Will and Orange Trucking might have a different opinion.

There are a few things we still need to work out. The truck died while I was creeping along going through a scale. It also does it during traffic jams, and when I'm backing. Will said the automatic engine shut off should only be activated when the breaks are pulled. Normally I would have heard over the CB 'White move that piece of shit out of the way, learn how to drive' Nobody said anything when I stalled. That was a nice change.

Never a dull moment at home either. Our son cut his hand pretty good / pretty bad, the other day. His girlfriend calls me and says, "Um, Leslie does Willis have like any insurance or anything"

Not yet, we are in between insurances, why, what happen.

"Well he like stabbed himself and we are here in ER"

WHAT! What Happen?

"Well he was trying to pry apart some frozen hamburger patties and the knife slipped and cut his hand, we have been here about an hour and they just took him back, he told me to call you"

Now at this point I was at least a little relieved to find out he only 'stabbed' his hand. And since he sat in the waiting room an hour seemed to me that the nurses did not think he would bleed to death or lose his hand.

But I was a little confused about why my genius engineering student could not figure out a better, safer way to separate hamburger. (I bet he can think of a better way now) When I talked to him later I reminded him that when I told him we were changing jobs we would have a 30 day wait before the new insurance starts, so no playing with fire or running with scissors. He said I said nothing about juggling knives. It's still too soon to tell if he will have any nerve damage or needs tendon repair surgery. The doctor thinks there might be tendon damage around his ring finger. Guess they will know more after they take the stitches out. I told him I hope this engineering thing works, since it's too late for him to become a piano prodigy. I have to take time to thank John our neighbor who drove Willy to the ER. I Need to see what special thank you treat I can find in my travels.

Well guess that's about all I have that's new. Just sitting here at Kimberly Clark in Jenks, Oklahoma waiting for our load to be ready. Waiting, waiting, waiting, some things never change.

Love and miss you all

The Honeymoon is over already?

It's so sad when the honeymoon ends.
We found out the hard way that Orange Trucking does not send you a HazMat route when they send you a HazMat load. Will says ever other company he worked for has sent hazmat approved routing. Heck even White did that, 1 point White Trucking.

Thank goodness Will was driving and not me. We had just switched drivers and we were on I95, near Baltimore, Maryland. And we see this sign that says last exit for HM. All HazMat must exit. Surprised, upset and confused Will exits. Next thing you know we are down town Baltimore.

DOWNTOWN BALTIMORE

We were on a street that has the light rail down the middle. There wasn't enough room for us to stay in our skinny lane so the driver's side of the truck and trailer was on the tracks. I decided to get dressed in case we had to jump out.   (I was in my pj's ready for bed)

Both the gps's and the qualcomm routing, kept telling us to turn at every street. But looking down each street it looked like there was a parking garage to drive under or a walking bridge or even smaller streets. I got the laptop up and looked like if we stay on Howard Street we will run into Martin Luther King JR and then we can turn left and takes us back onto the freeway and we can start over.

After we turn on MLK we pass Pennsylvania Avenue. And I started thinking. How close are we to the White House? Turns out we were only 38 miles away from the White House with a truck load of HazMat. Driving around where we are not allowed. HUM!!! And nobody stopped us.

Then I started to wonder how close we were to other interesting sites I would love to see in Baltimore. The USS Torsk Submarine 2 .5 miles. The USS Constellation Ship also 2.5 miles away. Edgar Allan Poe House and Museum, 1.3 miles away. Charm City Cakes, 2.3 miles. The Annabel Lee Tavern, 3.1 miles. The Annabel Lee is a very sad poem and is the last poem Edgar Allan Poe wrote. Annapolis,27 miles. Ok not nearby, but if I were driving I would have gotten lost there, accidently of course. I can't think of a better place to get lost where every day, is fleet week.

We had a little chat with our new DBL (driver business leader) and asked why they didn't send an HM route. He said all we have to do is call or check the map and route ourselves. Well fine now but maybe you should put a note on HM loads, double check your route. Will argued this point because when regulations and approved routes change and update, that information is sent to companies, NOT every individual driver. Orange Trucking's response was that's why we should call them. That takes a lot of time. Just send us a HM route. We told them White Trucking does but our dbl said that is not our policy.

After that we took a load from Pennsylvania to Logan, Utah. It's a refrigerated load. We tried to get out of it, telling them that we have no training in refer units, no experience. We talked to 3 different people they tried to give me refer training over the phone.

"Is the light green?"

No it's white.

"Well that's not right it should be green. Maybe the cover came off. What's the temp?"

I don't know where do I find that?

"Don't forget to put fuel in the refer unit itself."

Where does that go?

"You don't pay taxes on refer fuel, so it is pump separately."

"Call this number if you have any problems,"

I won't know there is a problem until it explodes, as I told the last 2 people I have no experience in refer unit. I was talking but they weren't listening

Well, the truth is, Will does have refer experience. But only a couple of times. He doesn't like them because it is hard to sleep with the refer unit turning on right next to the sleeper. It weighs 43,200. If we were owner op's and in our International Prostar, we could not take something that heavy.

But since it's not our fuel cost the only down side for us is the speed at which we will be crawling up the hills.

They routed a 43,000 pound load on 9-10% hills instead of the interstates. Orange Trucking figures why drive I 70 when US 40 runs right alongside of it.

US 40 through Pennsylvania is a beautiful scenic drive. For cars. Really beautiful for cars.

The road is not designed for semi-trucks. There is no room to pull over if I get a flat or whatever. I would be blocking the entire lane. Also it is just a two lane road. It goes through Union Town PA. I would have taken more pictures but I was busy practicing my down shifting.

There are little towns with stop lights at the bottom of step hills. 10% hills with a stop light at the bottom. This route would suck even if I was empty. The truck speed limit of 15 mph seemed like speeding sometimes.

We finally arrive and now it is time for some much needed time off. 34 hours off anyway. It's been a tough week with a steep learning curve, for me anyway.

Love and miss you all

A Post About Nothing.

Things I have learned while crusin' around the country side.

Truck driving is a hell of a way to make a living. It is impossible to succeed without support from family and friends.

No matter how hard you try, you cannot slam the curtain between the sleeper and the driver hard enough to convey enough anger and frustration. The Velcro only makes an angry sound when ripping open.

Don't drink the water in Yuma or El Paso. Don't brush your teeth. Don't even have orange juice with breakfast. It was obviously frozen and reconstituted with tap water. If you do, you might make it back to the hotel room, but not all the way to the bathroom.

The further east you drive the smaller the lanes get. Also the more people look twice at a female truck driver.

The radio should play more Runrig, John Butler Trio and Saffire the Upity Womans Blues.

Four-Wheelers need to learn how to merge. I can't stress enough how dangerous it is to not merge correctly. It is one of the most stressful parts of my driving day. Every time I approach an on ramp, I see a car, not paying attention, not looking, and just assuming the freeway will let them in. It is the vehicle that is merging into traffic has the responsibility to merge safely. It is not the traffic's responsibility to slam on our brakes so you can get on the freeway. Hang up the phone and drive. Accelerate and go in front or slow down and line up behind me. I know you know where your gas pedal is because when you try to squeeze in beside me as the merge lane ends you suddenly find your gas and your finger.... Stop It !

Everybody must make a trip to Memphis. Visit both Graceland and Beal Street. I would love to go back. Once was not enough. The history of music that has walked down that street is unbelievable. From rock stars, to Country singers, Jimmy Buffett and of course the Blues greats.

People, you do not _really_ want to see Nebraska, Wyoming, Iowa, the Dakota's, Arizona, Texas, No you don't! You only think you want to see all of America. I'll tell you what you're missing. Get a brown piece of paper, light brown, tan will do. Lay it on a table, put dirt and sand on the paper. There you go, you're on vacation in those states. OK, now let's go thru the seasons. Place the paper in front of a fan on high and now you're in Wyoming. Get the paper wet; place it in the freezer and now your experiencing Nebraska, Iowa, North and South Dakota, and Wyoming, in the fall.

Now put the frozen paper in front of that fan again, still on high, and you're in Wyoming again with old man winter.

Adult supervision is required to visit the next 2 states

Place the paper on your stove top, and now you are visiting Arizona and Texas, in the summer. There are tons of reasons NOT to go to Texas. In fact I understand there is an on line petition that

Texas wants to succeed from the union. Let them. I know where we can get boxes, we can all help them pack.

When I started this Will said I would only have to drive for 5 years. By then we would have the bills all paid and have enough money saved to buy a smaller house. One with a smaller tax bill, lower utilities, best of all NO HOUSE PAYMENT. Well, we have no car payments, no credit cards. Now all we need is a house. I have updated my housing requirements. Or lowered them depending on how you look at it. I'm willing to look at manufactured homes in a park. We wanted to stay away from that monthly space rent, but some of them include water, sewer, and garbage. And most of the manufactured homes don't need a lot of work, mostly paint and carpeted.

We will be home for Christmas. Santa is bringing me a granddaughter. Jennifer and her husband are expecting baby girl #4 on Dec 22. In between holding the new granddaughter, last minute shopping, Christmas dinner at our house, spending time with family, catching up with friends, cleaning the house, see the other grandkids, I hope we have time to look at houses. Both stick built and manufactured.

I know this was probably a boring post. You can read my previous posts if you get too bored.

Love and miss you all

Oh Dear, Deer!!

I'm driving through Spokane Washington after picking up paper rolls in Pomeroy Washington, and it is icy and slippery. Paper rolls suck. Icy roads suck. Together they bite. Spokane is a hilly town, and you have to go through Main Street to get to the freeway I 84. Think of San Francisco with ice. The paper rolls are HEAVY. They are top heavy. They shift easily. Each roll weighs 7665 pounds and we have 6 rolls. YUCK! Did I mention paper rolls suck.   Everyone is driving slowly because of the sheet of ice on the road. What snow was on the road yesterday froze overnight and now it is freezing rain. CRAP! But at least people around here know this is dangerous and they are all driving extra carefully, and no one is flipping me off for driving so slow.

I get to one section of road without any stop signs or stop lights and everyone is stopping, or at least trying to because there are a heard of deer crossing the road. Cars stop and let one pass then they go. It's like the deer think they are supposed to take turns. Anyway I get up to where they are crossing; I already heard warning of it on the CB. They are crossing from my right to left. One deer is standing on the left side off the road, and two does are hanging out in the medium between traffic, and three does are coming from the right side of the road. I can't stop because I am headed up hill; I would slowly slide backwards downhill. CRAP! CRAP!!

Two deer fall right in front of me. I hate to use the visual aid of Bambi on ice, but that's exactly what it looked like. I didn't feel anything so maybe they made it. No they didn't, Will said he saw the car behind me try to stop but hit one deer after I hit it. YUCK! I feel so bad.

The guys on the CB were all joking. "Hey driver looks like you're leaving a lot of jerky on the road". "That's a two-fer, nice shooting Tex". After we got out of town we pulled over and Will got out and looked to see if there was any damage to the front of the truck or the radiator and to make sure there wasn't anything stuck under the truck.

I love and miss you all

3rd Times the Charm

I cannot believe it took 3 tries to drug test Will.

Last month we sat for 10 hours without a load. I kept sending in messages with no response. Oh sure my messages started off polite but of course that never lasts long.

We are empty, and ready for a load please. We have been empty for 1 hour ready for a load. 2 hrs sitting need load. Do you know you have a team truck sitting without a load. Hello is this thing on. If there are no loads send me home.

I will say that one big difference between White Trucking and Orange Trucking is White Trucking would usually answer me. Our DM (driver manager) would say stuff like the freight gods are just not cooperating with us today, or freight is low in your area. Etc., sometimes she would say something stupid, practically setting me up, and I would think to myself, you do not know who you are sparing with. I know you don't know me or my family but sarcasm is a competition sport for us. I don't mean to brag, but I do hold the most gold medals. My dramatic combination eye rolling and sighing is trademarked. As my former employers and co-workers will swear to, and have mentioned in all my farewell cards. But not Orange Trucking. No response from them, no matter how my messages evolved. While White Trucking's unwritten policy must be poke the bear, enrage the driver. Orange Trucking's policy must be let the driver vent don't engage the rage.

So the second time they attempted a drug test was on our trip from Sacramento to Tampa Florida. After we started they sent us a message to stop in Houston. That's 107 miles out of route. Gee I wonder why. Oh I guess I should let you know that the drug tests are random and secret. They can only inform you like 30 min or some short period of time, just to give you enough time to get from where you are to the lab. They don't want to give you any time to get any clean urine off the black market. So I hurry getting to Houston, because I was almost out of hours for the day and we should be changing drivers before Houston, but did not want to waste the time. We figured we would just change drivers while Will is doing his drug test. Changing drivers takes about 30min. Post trip, pre trip inspections, bathroom breaks, dinner, shower, fuel etc., whatever it is we try to do it during our driver changes.

Anyway about 3 hours from the Houston Terminal they send me a message, looks we will be gone when you get there, just stay and call us at 6am pst –they are in Fontana California. I sent back a message asking why? We need to deliver this load by Saturday in Florida and stopping overnight in Houston means that won't happen. We are not out here on vacation, there is nothing I want to do or see in Houston. (DUH everybody knows that) We need these miles on this check. (Well that is my go to excuse; always need these miles on that check) The only response is stay put call in am.

There is nothing at the Houston Terminal. It's a dump. It is full of stinky oil tankers. Hard to even find a spot for a 53 foot van. There is no grill. Funny how fast we got used to that little perk, most of the terminals have a grill. There were not even any food flyers. How are we supposed to order dinner? We call at 6am and the DBL asked us, "When you guys start driving again, who will drive first?"

I said, same schedule as always, I drive about 4am-4pm, Will drives 4pm -4am. There is a little silence on the other end and then he says, "Oh then that's not going to work, um yea that's not going to work, ok sorry. Never mind."

That is when I lost it.

WHAT! ARE YOU KIDDING ME? NEVER MIND! YOU HOLD US HERE FOR 14 HOURS FOR NOTHING. YOU COST US GETTING 6300 MILES FOR THE WEEK.

The dbl (he who shall not be named) said," I'm sorry, I know how you feel"

OH NO SIR, DON'T YOU DARE SAY THAT. OBVIOUSLY YOU DO NOT KNOW HOW I FEEL, SORRY DOESN'T FIX OUR MILES THIS WEEK. SORRY DOESNT PAY US FOR SITTING. IF YOU'RE BOSS TOLD YOU TO COME IN AND SIT AT YOUR DESK AND DO NOTHING FOR 14 HOURS WOULDN'T YOU EXPECT TO GET PAID. WE NEED TO BE COMPENSATED FOR THIS FORCED SITTING TIME. WHY DO YOU GUYS MAKE IT SO HARD TO GET A UA FROM THE NIGHT SHIFT DRIVER? THAT'S WHAT THIS WAS ALL ABOUT RIGHT?

IF ONLY THERE WAS SOME WAY TO GET A LIST OF ALL THE HOSPITALS IN THE UNITED STATES WITH A LAB, PLACES WHERE WE COULD GO GET A DRUG TEST DONE. YOU DO HAVE INTERNET THERE DON'T YOU. WOULD IT BE EASIER IF I SET UP AN APPOINTMENT.

HELL EVEN WHITE TRUCKING HAS THAT FIGURED OUT.

I am pacing the floor, back and forth. At some point Will left, he always refuses to watch my self imposed implosions. I managed to empty out most of the drivers lounge too. After taking a breath, I said to the dbl, I know you are not to blame you are just the lucky recipient of my frustration, feel free to convey my anger to anyone you want. Please forward this taped

~ 218 ~

phone conversation on up the chain of command. In fact I hope you do.

The third time was today. About 2 hours after we changed drivers, Will is just about in laa-laa land. A couple arthritis pills some Benadryl and good night Will. I got a message, "When you get to Mattoon IL, pull over to safe location and call in they need to talk to Will, Yes we know he is in the sleeper but please wake him, we need to talk to him."

Great I get to poke the Bear, and I'm not even lost this time. Will asks her, she who shall not be named, if he is supposed to come up on his logs for this. She said, "Well some of our drivers prefer not to and some do, it's up to you."

Ok that's what Will wanted to hear. He really thinks he is supposed to log this drug test as working not driving time, because it is something the company has ordered you to do, something you are legally required to do. Like putting on chains in bad weather, or like taking a class etc. but she says not logging it is ok, then OK. They send us to the Mattoon Hospital. There are 3 buildings and we pick the first one. Will goes up to the desk and tells the nurse, that Orange Trucking sent him here for a UA. She says, "What, what's that?", the other nurse says, "Oh you mean a drug screen? That's over in the other building"

We go. He pee's. We're done.

Now those that don't know me may think that is the end of it. But if they did not care about getting the test done during Will's driving time, why did they have us sit in Houston? If Will did not have to come up on his logs to show his drug test, why did they waste our time twice before? Time is money. Why did it take 3 times to figure this out? Is Will your first and only night time driver?

Will said I could not message them about that. He said he was putting his foot down. (It's cute when he does that)

Whatever,*currently rolling my eyes**

Love and miss you all

Another Wrong Turn, are you kidding me

I don't know if police regular pull trucks over here in Pharr Texas, or if it was because it was Friday. There were 3 trucks pulled over. One right after another. It can't be for speeding. The speed limit in Texas is 70 for trucks, except at night, its 65. Unless you're a car then its 75.

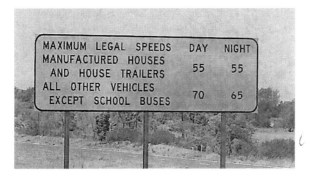

Except at night then its 70, unless you are a passenger bus then its 75 except at night then its 65, unless you are a car towing something then its 70 except at night then its 65. Except during road construction then its 45 and don't forget 'headlights on when wipers are needed.' I think that about sums it all up. Ron White does this bit about the Texas speed limits; it's funnier when he does it.

I bent the internet connector thingy. It still works, but just going to cost us more money. We are going to have to replace it before it dies at the worst possible moment. Which you know it will. When Will needs the computer. I can hear it thinking now. Waiting until I take a wrong turn, and that's when it will strike. The internet won't work. It won't be a quite ending either. Ripping out and stomping all over someone's last nerve is never silent or pretty.

When I woke up this morning we were still in Texas. We are about 900 miles from our destination. I get to stay on I35 north for a long time. Thru the little bit of Texas that's left, Oklahoma, Kansas, Missouri and Iowa. Then it should be Wills shift. Easy money today. Not so fast you're getting ahead of me.

When I get into Kansas I get on the turn pike. I carefully followed Wills written instructions. He is getting more and more specific with directions. While on **I 35north** in Kansas I take **exit 127**. Good deal. Then as I get into Wichita I am supposed to take **I 435 east**. It goes around the city and has less traffic. Then on the other side of the city I get on **I 35east**. I do that, now I am on **435east**. Then at one point the freeway splits I can either take **I 435**north, or 470 **east**

~~queue jeopardy music da-da-da-da-da-da-dot-da-da-da-da-da~~

Alex, I'll take stay with easterly direction for $1000.

Oh sorry, the correct answer is stay with numbers **435**.

Will is up and says **WHAT DID YOU DO?**

First off, how does he know the minute I screw up? I said "Nothing I stayed straight",

WELL IT'S WRONG YOU SHOULD BE ON 435 EAST.

(a ha I got you now...in my head) There was no **435 east** it was either 470 **east** or **435** North.

HOW MANY TIMES DO I HAVE TO TELL YOU EAST AND NORTH ARE THE SAME?

(I guess one more time. In my head)

WHERE DOES IT SAY TAKE 470 EAST,

Where does it say to take **435 North**.

YOU SHOULD KNOW THAT BY NOW! COMING UP YOU'RE GOING TO HAVE TO TAKE A ROAD THAT I DIDNT WRITE DOWN, IT'S A CONNECTING ROAD THAT TAKES YOU TO THE ROAD WE NEED. I

THOUGHT YOU COULD DO THAT BY NOW

~~Ding, Ding, Ding. The daily double, ~~

Alex, I'd like to bet it all on 'not a snow ball's chance in hell'

Remember look for my body off route. Luckily I didn't have to try. My shift is thankfully over. 652 miles. Will can take it from here. We deliver in about 4 hours and they haven't sent us a reload yet. We were afraid of that happening. They must have something in the yard we can take. I know that made me laugh too, but we can always hope. We have together close to 50 hours left to work this week. But looks like we are going to be in Minnesota for the weekend, resetting our hours, when we don't need too.

Love and miss you all

AARP I Think Not

Many of you felt a disturbance in the force last night, in case you missed it, both Will and I were given the senior dinner discount.

WTH! Only one of us qualifies for that and it is not me. I just don't get it? I pay good money for this hair color. I was raised a good Irish, Catholic girl. I never did drugs. I never smoked. I say please and thank you. I even have karma points in the bank to ward off bad things like this happening to me. AARP doesn't even have my address yet, actually they do but it's for Will.

Well little Miss Suzie Q waitress just aced herself out of a tip. Will thought it was funny and tipped her anyway.

Love and miss you all

Mi Casino su Casino

Since I don't have a lot of 'lost' story's I thought I would give you my 2cents about casinos. If I were to list the all the casino's we have been too you would think we had a gambling problem. But what the heck I'll give you a good list anyway. In no particular order, they are;

Argosy Casino in Kansas City Missouri. Without a doubt the best food of any casino we ever went to. We had to take a taxi from our hotel in Kansas City Kansas. You have got to Google this one. It is set up as if you were walking into a castle courtyard. The ceiling is painted like a sky at dawn or dusk. The gambling sections are set up like villagers might be selling yarn or baskets. But like I said the best part was the food, we didn't even care we lost while there.

Route 66 Casino, Albuquerque, NM lots of fun. Rolling Hills in Corning, CA. and 7-Feathers, Canyonville, OR. Are both good places to stop. You have to stop at the truck stop for 7 Feathers then take the shuttle but the buffet is decent. Rolling Hills was good to Will but I never had much luck there.

Fire Keepers, Battle Creek MI. We had to take a taxi to this one from the truck stop. There was another driver going too so we split the taxi. I had good luck at the roulette table there.

Nugget Casino, Wendover NV. Winnemucca Casino, Winnemucca NV We always had good luck here, if you can get past the cigarettes Will likes the older Bally Machines.

Hollywood Casino, Toledo OH. This one was probably the most entertaining. The staff was dressed up as famous people. I saw Gene Simmons dealing Black Jack. Cindy Lauper running the bar (Time after time is my favorite song of hers), Arnold Schwarzenegger in the Poker room. I wish I played poker, but counting to 21 is stressful enough.

The Muckleshoot Casino in Auburn, WA has a great buffet and fun roulette tables. You have to take a taxi from your hotel but it's fun.

Kla-Mo-Ya Casino, in Chiloquin OR not a good place to eat but the slots aren't bad. It's a good place to park it for the night in bad weather or just to change drivers.
Double Eagle in Cripple, Creek CO. Tachi Casino in Lemoore, CA. The Virgin River Casino in Mesquite, NV, Eldorado Casino in Reno, NV. Apache in Globe, AZ. The Lovelock Casino in Lovelock, NV, Wildhorse inPendleton, OR. The Horseshoe Casino in Council Bluffs, Iowa. The Apache Nugget in Cuba, NM. And Sams Town, Las Vegas.

Casinos are great places for truck drivers. They have parking and a buffet with a

salad bar. It is very frustrating when we deliver to a business and then we are not allowed to park there. Many Wal-Mart's have no semi parking signs. REALLY! If you don't want us parking there I guess I'll go somewhere else and spend my money. But it really sucks when you need supplies and have to pay truck stop prices. Life would be a lot easier if everyone would remember one thing;
IF YOU BOUGHT IT, A TRUCK BROUGHT IT
Well gotta go make some money to cover our losses.

Love and miss you all.

No Problem, They are Made to Break Away

Will pulls in to get fuel and as always I run to the bathroom. On my way back to the truck, I pass Will headed in and he throws me the keys and says he couldn't wait. Now normally if we are both up our fuel routine goes like this. Will pumps the fuel, I go in and use the restroom, when I'm done I return to the truck so Will can go in. I pull the truck forward so the guy behind me can fuel, then I go in and see what they have in the gift shop, get water, postcards etc. Then we both go back to the truck continue on our merry way. That being said, I followed our routine. But Will did not. I pulled the truck about 2 feet before I heard a POP, well first I felt a little tug but just thought I was in a rut and gave it a little more gas. Then I heard the POP.

I looked in my mirrors and saw the diesel fuel hose no longer attached to the pump, but hanging from my fuel tank. CRAP. So I run inside and even thou there is a line of drivers I cut in front and say, quietly, that I am at pump 27 and I pulled the hose out of the pump. The guy called maintenance and the girl followed me out to the pumps. She had the hose reconnected before the maintenance guy showed up but since there wasn't any fuel spilled they didn't need him.

I didn't go in to meet Will. I didn't want to face the humiliating snickers from the other drivers. But I told Will when he got back to the truck and you know what he said. "I heard something about that, but didn't think anything until they said the Orange Truck driver, then I figured it was you."

Love and miss you all

Hum, Texas

I saw a church called, The Overcoming Faith Christian Center. Maybe that's where you go to be deprogrammed when you move to Texas as a Catholic.

What is the problem with pick up or delivery in Texas and Oklahoma? Something always goes wrong. One business address was off by a few years. The guard said, they moved to this bigger warehouse a couple of years ago, but I guess no one has changed it in the computer yet. Another address was towards a housing development and our directions specifically warned us that if you miss your turn, do not turn into the housing development, they <u>will</u> call the police and they <u>will</u> give you a very pricey ticket, which you <u>will</u> pay out of your own pocket. So why don't you give the drivers better directions? Besides, I don't know why they put fancy houses near the Kimberly Clark paper mill anyway. That is a sticky place to live.

Another problem is road signs. My instructions said turn on 820 west. Ok I think I'm getting close because I pass the ramp for 820 north. About 30 minutes later I tell Will, I think I should have turned on to 820 west by now. After looking around he tells me I passed it. Oh no I did not! I was looking very carefully. I even turned down the radio so my eyes would work better. He says I should have taken the ramp for 820 north. I tried to explain that north is not west. He said it is when you're in Texas, and for future directions, south is east and visa-versa. One time I was on interstate 10 south, we needed I 610. Off to the right on a big overhead sign with a big arrow we see Spur 281. (Or whatever the number was) somehow we should have known that Texas 281 spur was the connecting road to I 610. And of course taking the next exit to turn around is no simple task.

We did get to drive by Willie Nelson's place. Bio- Willie. It's a bar, truck stop, gift shop. He supports local biodiesel alternative fuel. Its in a little town called Carls Corner,

This last load was from Huston Texas to Logan Utah. We picked it up at a Wal-Mart warehouse. It didn't weight anything 5,000 pounds so we like those loads. We get better fuel mileage that way.

We deliver and find out this place is just disposing of the whole truck load. It is toys that have too much lead to sell. Cloth bowling pin and ball set.

When we arrive the business is closed but there is another driver already waiting. When the employees arrive in the morning, they unloaded him first. They just  threw his load in the dumpster. They started to do the same to our load but the dumpster quickly filled up and they asked if we could follow them to the city landfill so they would finish unloading. We got permission from our dispatch and off we went.

Our time is up, we've each worked 70 hours this week. It's time to rest, do laundry, go shopping for supplies, sleep in a real bed for one night, watch a tv that doesn't go all screwy when a truck drives by and interrupts the reception and most importantly, abuse the shower. I take one when I get to the hotel, before bed, when I wake up, and before we check out. Oh yeah, as many hot showers as I want for as long as I want. Hey at $20 per shower at the truck stops, I'm making darn sure I get my money's worth at the hotel.

We Quit!

We are home and have accomplished most, of our goals as team drivers. We learned a lot about each other and ourselves. And confirmed some of what we already knew. You wouldn't think after nearly 30 years together there would be anything else to learn.

We set off needing to get caught up on bills while I was unemployed, and also wanted to get a smaller place to live. One that would not require both of us to work full time to maintain. We accomplished that. We bought a 3 bedroom, 2 bath home. We completely remodeled it. We have no house payment. We have no car payments. We have no credit cards.

I learned that Will loves truck driving no matter how much he complains about it. He has driven 32 years, approximately 3 million miles under his belt with no accidents, and only a couple of tickets, in California, an extremely rare feat. I couldn't manage that in my short 5 year career. He is an excellent driver. He is an excellent backer. He does not get himself into situations that he cannot get out of.

I'm not sure if I can say what Will learned from me. He certainly knows what I can and cannot eat. He always knew my directional short comings, but perhaps is a little more concerned when I go out shopping now, afraid I may not make it home.

I don't have any regrets. Truck driving allowed me to have experiences I never would have had, and will never forget. I saw weather we don't have in Oregon. I got to meet interesting people, very interesting. The majority of truck drivers are great. They are safe drivers. They are helpful and respectful. Just like any group of people there is just the 2% that give the others a bad name. I actually feel safer getting out in the middle of the night to walk to the bathroom at a truck stop than I do at a road side rest area.

We chose to start driving with White Trucking because they offer a great program where the husband can train the wife. That meant I did not have to go off with a trainer for 2 to 3 months. Getting someone to understand my IBS would have been extremely personal. Even though I mention it in here I didn't dwell on the daily jogs to a bathroom. After what we just refer to as "the incident" Will and I have an understanding that if I did not come back from a bathroom in a reasonable length of time, Will would grab a pair of sweat pants and bring them to me in the lady's room. Usually there is someone walking out that can bring them to me. I couldn't drink coffee unless we were at a hotel for our 34 off. I gave up soda and that helped a little. I could never eat salad unless we were staying overnight. Fast food was always out of the question for me.

We spent more time with Orange Trucking than the couple of stories here suggest. There was just not that much to complain about and when I did they were usually resolved. So no extra venting was necessary

Truck driving allowed me to see amazing sites. I've been from sea to shining sea. I've see the spacious skies of Montana. And the Dakota's. The amber waves of grain in America's heartland, and the purple mountain majesties of the west coast.

Montgomery & Selma Alabama. Gettysburg, Pennsylvania. Four Corners New Mexico. Tornado damage in Joplin Missouri. Wounded Knee, South Dakota.

Driving thru Sturgis, SD made both of us long for our Harley days. Seeing the aftermath of a pick-up vs 3 bike wreck gave us pause to rethink. Changing lanes and freeways in New York and New Jersey had me swearing like, well, a truck driver and thanking God that I didn't live there. Seeing the beautiful country side of upstate New York and Connecticut had me thankful I was able to enjoy the view.

Searching for a trailer in a railyard in Houston provided me several nominees for the annual Darwin awards. Seeing a sunrise in Moab, Utah made me thank God for giving me the opportunity to see something so beautiful.

I safely and successfully drove on some notorious hills. Notorious to truckers anyway. I can proudly buy and wear a t-shirt that says "I survived…" Donner Pass, CA. The Grapevine, CA. Tehachapi, CA. Cabbage Hill, OR. Siskiyou Pass, CA, OR. Loveland Pass, NV.

Union Pass, AZ. Teton Pass, WY. Vail Pass, CO. Cajon Pass, CA. Port Matilda Hill, PA.

It's time to start writing Chapter 11 of our life, Semi-retirement.

Since we have been home we have been able to be there for the birth of 2 more grandchildren. Our grandson comes over after school just to hang out with grandpa.

I now get paid to babysit my grand-daughters. Jennifer doesn't know I would do it for free. I also get to work with my brother in his catering business. I am extremely blessed.

I come home to a clean house, dinner and a glass of wine every night and that makes life good, very good.

Leslie

I put in a section of photographs. Pictures of interesting signs, and other special sights. After all a picture is worth a thousand words, and turns out it's cheaper to print too.

I could not put in all my pictures. I choose to not include the pictures that really only work in color. Like pictures of Moab Utah, everyone should get on line and check it out. The red rocks and scenery deserves to be seen in color or in person. There was really no reason to include all my bad weather pictures. Snow does not look impressive in black and white. The glow from a forest fire is not striking unless in color. But I hope you enjoy the ones I did include.

If you wish to view more pictures in color please visit

lesliesemiview.blogspot.com/2013/08/pictures-from-our-travels.html

If you wish to contact me please do at Oursemiview2013@Gmail.com

Waiting to be loaded at FedEx

That's a lot of Bull

Armadillo at Texas rest stop

Fort Stockton, Texas Welcoming Committee cutouts

El Paso Border Patrol
check point.

Bales of Cotton

I can't remember where this is, I think Utah,
beautiful
red
rocks

A plane traveling by ground rather than air

Above the clouds at
Donner Pass

Cool cloud over Mount Shasta I took
this picture from the little space between the
side mirror on the left and the window post on
the right.

The shoe tree,
near Shaniko
Oregon.

That's a lot of
garlic headed
up Grapevine
in California

Driving
in
Montana

Montana

Mount
Ashland
in Oregon
also the
cover
photo

Very Icy roads in Wisconsin

Plate says
I M 35

~ 241 ~

Looks like I can get all my Christmas shopping done at one store this year.

A little construction fun

Sign at the Laredo Yard

Trying something new with the camera

Stanton Texas

AASHO road test site In Illinois

Rest stop in Moab, Utah

TRUCKERS YOU ARE NOT DOWN YET
ANOTHER 1½ MILES OF STEEP GRADES
AND SHARP CURVES TO GO

And Will wonders how I get
lost so easily

Route 666 near Shiprock NM, I could not reach my Rosary beads, so I just said a prayer to my patron saint, St Anne

Happy to be green

Chunky Mississippi

A rest area in Missouri

Girls gone Wild Bus next to an Oregon Ducks RV

Rock Creek Lodge in Clinton Montana

Don't worry we were parked

Will waiting patiently for traffic

Shiprock, New Mexico

Moab
Utah

Another truck with breaks on fire at the bottom
of the Grapevine grade in California

Penelope the dragon on I 5 near Yreka California

A church next to a tobacco field

Waiting for
trailer repairs
in Florida

The State of Jefferson is between Oregon and
California

A Weigh
Station sign
I can't miss

Mt. Shasta

Home
Sweet
Home

Acknowledgments

My sincere thanks to my extraordinary family. Whether they knew it or not they had to take turns giving me encouragement to continue driving and later to write some of it down here. They stepped in when my kids needed a mom and I couldn't be there. When I realized reading my bible would not be enough, my mom gave me more spiritual support than I thought I would need.

My extended family and friends. Even if we had to communicate through email and post cards, I could feel your support. Thanks to my cousin Thurman Banks for your tips on writing and publishing. I feel like you, writing your book was a stepping stone for me.

My remarkable kids, Paige, Jennifer and Willis. Every parent wants their kids to do better than they did. You all have soared past our dreams and continue to amaze us. Thanks for making me feel needed, even though I know you could do this all on your own.

And last but certainly not least my husband Will. Thanks for letting me invade your world. You told me time and time again to "Suck it up! There is NO crying in truck driving". But eventually there were times you joined me. The experience was unforgettable. I hope you enjoyed the ride as much as I did. I can't wait to see where life sends us next.

Guess what, a couple more blank pages.

~ 251 ~

Last one, I promise

~ 252 ~

CPSIA information can be obtained at www.ICGtesting.com
Printed in the USA
LVOW06s1935290915

456208LV00001B/43/P

9 781490 453040